DEFENCE IN THE NUCLEAR AGE

DEFENCE IN THE NUCLEAR AGE

by

STEPHEN KING-HALL

LONDON
VICTOR GOLLANCZ LTD
1958

© *K.-H. Services Ltd, 1958*

First published March 1958
Second impression before publication

Printed in Great Britain by
The Camelot Press Ltd., London and Southampton

"The day of the Lord will come as a thief in the night: in which the heavens shall pass away with a great noise and the elements shall melt with fervent heat, the earth also and the words that are therein shall be burned up."

2 Peter iii. 10

"Many a victory has been and will be suicidal to the victors."

Plato

"Peace cannot be kept by force. It can only be achieved by understanding."

Einstein

CONTENTS

FOREWORD

THE BOOK YOU are about to read is a discussion about national defence in the nuclear age. The issues confronting every human being in this matter are both simple and perplexing. Simple, because they are easy to understand; perplexing because all possible solutions are fraught with great known and unknown risks. What's to be done?

After examining the whole question in an objective manner I have reached the conclusion that the balance of advantage lies in the declaration (unilaterally if necessary) by the British Government that the United Kingdom will abandon the use of nuclear energy for military purposes. Such a decision, as explained in the book, would lead to momentous consequences, some good, some full of risk. It would profoundly affect the size of our conventional forces and our relations with the U.S.A.; on the other hand it would release powerful forces and resources for the political warfare aspect of defence.

I suspect from discussion whilst this book was being written that many experts in defence will declare that, whereas they concede the validity of a great deal of what is to be found in Parts I and II of the book, Part III is more than they can stomach and they will conclude that I have "gone pacifist". In short, that a strategy of defence and *attack* against Soviet directed communism which is not based on violence is necessarily "Pacifist", a word which to many people conveys an attitude of Christian resignation and of turning the other cheek. Admirable as this attitude may be, it is not the policy particularly recommended in this book. The object of the strategy outlined in this volume is not only to defend our way of life but to destroy Communism. I reject as being anything more than an uneasy armistice all wishful thinking that there can be "peaceful co-existence" in the one-world of today between Communism and the democratic way of life.

Mr George Kennan in his B.B.C. Reith lectures drew attention to the importance of a correct appreciation of the nature of a Soviet strategy in which armed force plays a secondary part, but because Mr Khrushchev appears to understand the limitations of violence we should not consider him to be a "Pacifist". What we must do is to beat the Communists in the strategy and tactics of Total War in the nuclear age. In order to do this we must secure the political and economic initiative and this is not best done by competing in a nuclear arms race. This highly perilous policy suffers from the fatal defect that since we shall never inaugurate a nuclear preventive war it is at the best a purely defensive strategy lacking that element of attack which is the best method of defence.

Our policy must do more than deter the Communist leaders; it must defeat them in the world wide struggle for the allegiance of men's minds, and do so without the peril of the sudden destruction of all we wish to defend.

I call upon those who after reading this book are still unable to make that complete break through the thought-barrier needed in a situation in which, as I write these words, a Russian satellite is circling the globe, to give their support to an authoritative enquiry into the whole question raised in these pages. Nothing less will do, though much more than that should be done.

STEPHEN KING-HALL, 1957

The Penthouse,
162 Buckingham Palace Road,
London

I acknowledge with gratitude the assistance I have received from Miss Ann King-Hall in the preparation of this book.

INTRODUCTION

In KING-HALL NEWS-LETTER Number 475 of 16th August, 1945, published after the first atomic bombs had fallen on Hiroshima and Nagasaki, I wrote:

"We are now living in the age of controlled atomic energy . . . the most revolutionary event which has yet occurred in the history of man . . . the news of the collapse of Japan . . . is of very little significance as measured by the standards of what the Atomic Bomb is going to mean to mankind.

"I say the Atomic Bomb and do not refer to the use of atomic energy for peaceful purposes because . . . at least ten years are likely to elapse before atomic energy can be used for non-war-like purposes . . . those two bombs . . . may have been and I think will prove to have been the last explosions of consequence in the history of large scale war. Total war—large scale national war—is at an end. It has vanished from the sphere of practical politics . . . physical violence as a continuation of political purposes will be limited to riots and large scale police action. . . . Total War has reached its ultimate and absolute physical development, it has made political and economic nationalism a meaningless thing and so Total War has abolished itself . . . (but) it does not seem as if the obvious fact that Total War has become meaningless is yet fully understood. . . . Three great powers, the U.S.A., Great Britain and Russia will soon be able to make atomic bombs; they will be joined by France, Sweden and others. The manufacture of the bombs will become easier. What then? It is impossible to imagine that the nations or the masses will tolerate a situation in which at the slightest ruffle on the waters of international politics people will say: 'Suppose they send over a hundred atomic bombers tonight?' No national state will ever dare issue an ultimatum to another with a time limit of even six hours, because the reply in five hours might be a shower of A.B.'s. It is obviously a situation which cannot remain in a state of suspended animation. Something will have to be done about it. . . . The Atomic Bomb enables its user to strike with devastating and comprehensive effect at the whole of the enemy's civil population. Whoever uses it *first* does not necessarily *win the war* because the atomic bombers of nation A may be on their way to bomb nation B whilst their own homeland is being turned into a crematorium. Both sides may more or less simultaneously knock each other out of the ring. . . ."

Twelve years later I saw no reason to modify the conclusions reached in 1945 but it was alarmingly clear that my conviction that "something will have to be done about it" had been over-optimistic. Nothing had been done about it and mankind appeared to be in a kind of schismatic condition as it watched in paralysed alarm the progress of its scientists in the task of projecting packaged explosions of enormous and literally unimaginable violence via the stratosphere from one part of the globe to another.

It was twelve years after News-Letter 475 that I published News-Letter 1083 and its sequel 1087. The heading was "Reflections on Defence". The conclusion of the arguments outlined in these news-letters was that our defence policy, as set forth in the Government's White Paper on Defence 1957, was based on the existence of a weapon—the H-bomb—which had two serious defects. First, that although in 1957 the best scientific opinion did not agree as to the amount of harm which was being done to the future of humanity from the fall-out consequent upon test explosions, all the experts agreed that if the tests were continued indefinitely some harm and perhaps serious evils were certain.[1] It is right to add that in 1957 there was talk of successful experiments designed to produce a clean bomb. This was not really "good news".

The second and, to my way of thinking, most serious defect of the H-bomb is that experimental data provide proof that this weapon, with whose existence our defence policy is linked, would, if ever used, lead to the certain destruction of everything we desire to defend.

For these and other reasons it was clear to me that our defence policy, based as it was on the traditional foundation of using force for defence against force, was open to serious criticism.

[1] See various reports including that of Joint Congressional Committee on Atomic Energy on radio-active fall-out and its effects on man.

I therefore suggested that it was desirable to consider whether it was possible for our defence policy to be based on a different foundation and whether there was any other form of defence against aggression which could be adopted.

If the use of force involved the acceptance of so many objectionable conditions, uncertainties and possibilities, what about the practice of non-violence as a basis for our defence policy?

Merely to ask such a question causes bewilderment in many minds. The whole idea is novel and almost absurd to any person who has never thought of defence except in terms of violence. But the H-bomb is also novel and horribly, obscenely, absurd. During the past century many ideas which intelligent men in 1860 would have regarded as fantastic have become accepted as part of our daily lives. It is unlikely that the man of 1860 would have either believed or understood a prophet who told him: "Your grandson will fly at 500 miles an hour, see pictures and hear voices from afar as easily as you hear or see me as I talk to you in this room; he will invent a bomb of which six would destroy London, and he will send a satellite round the world."

It is unreasonable to suppose that the whole subject of defence and the traditional ideas associated with it cannot be subject to revolutionary changes. It would be a very exceptional form of human activity if it escaped the revolution which has transformed civilization in the past few decades.

Defence has been revolutionized materially but remained mentally stagnant. Some aspects of defence had undergone remarkable changes before the arrival of the nuclear weapon and all the nuclear weapon has done is to enormously accelerate tendencies already becoming noticeable in the pre-nuclear age. We must break through the thought-barrier in defence thinking and see what we find on the other side, a thought-barrier represented by the centuries old idea of most people that violence is the only practical means of defence against violence.

"Most people" did not and does not include the Pacifists who up till now have had a monopoly of the idea that violence may not be the only way of countering violence. The Pacifist is not interested in countering violence, he is concerned with his conviction that violence as such is morally wrong. The conscientiously held views of the Pacifist—and I am bound to say I think they have the teachings of Jesus on their side—command my deep respect and admiration but it would be untrue to report that I have been able to share and translate into action moral pacifist ideas during the two world wars in which I have taken part.

I am not a Pacifist in the accepted sense of that word and do not feel any sense of guilt or shame on looking across my study and contemplating a case of medals acquired by four generations of my family, from 1812 onwards, in consideration of our efforts to slaughter the enemies of Britain in time of war. But I see no reason why opinions held by Pacifists for moral causes are therefore necessarily to be ignored by non-Pacifists if such opinions are useful for defence purposes.

I therefore suggested in News-Letter 1083 of 24th April, 1957 that we should take a new look at our defence arrangements and that, as part of this process, there should be a Royal Commission, or perhaps a committee sponsored by the Imperial Defence College, charged with the task of looking into the advantages and disadvantages of non-violent resistance as the basis of our national defence policy.

If such an enquiry showed that such a basis was better than our present one, whose unsatisfactory character I have outlined, then morality and expediency would find themselves on the same platform and I saw no harm in that possible result.

II

On September 10th, 1947 the *Manchester Guardian* published a letter from me which included the following remarks:

"The reports now reaching this country of the physical destruction caused by the release of the atomic bomb confirm to the fullest extent the estimate of those who declared that this event signalled a turning-point in human affairs.

"If national sovereignty is not subordinated to some effective form of international control an unprecedented disaster in human history is sure to take place. . . .

". . . When the bomb fell the most unimaginative people were momentarily stirred into awareness of the need for quick and drastic action. Nothing happened; apathy resumed its sway. I therefore propose:

"(a)   That the Government suggest that a joint Parliamentary Congressional Select Committee be appointed forthwith to report to Parliament and Congress upon the consequences and implications of the bomb.

"(b)   That the Government propose that when this report is completed the members of the British Houses of Parliament—or a full committee thereof composed of not less than 400 M.P.s and 100 Peers—proceed to Washington together with the Speaker and Lord Chancellor for a five-day joint Congressional-Parliamentary debate on the recommendations of the report.

"If this plan were to be adopted the ordinary man in the street would say: 'At last something has happened in the political world which measures up to the scope of the bomb.'

"All this may be unusual, but so is an atomic bomb."

These suggestions were ignored and "the plumed horrors" of radio-active clouds began to become commonplace, first in the Pacific areas and then in Siberia. The tactical nuclear weapon was developed and bedevilled the situation.

However, when I returned to the subject in 1957 I was astonished by the widespread response to a proposal (for an enquiry) put forward in a small circulation news-letter.

Naturally, the Pacifist publications in Britain and overseas welcomed my suggestion which, they were careful to point out, came from a person with "a military background". I had the impression that I was regarded as a butcher turned vegetarian! But I must acknowledge my debt to *Peace News* and other Pacifist papers because they at once canvassed non-Pacifists and thus revealed a wide measure of support for the idea of an enquiry from people who, though not Pacifists in the moral sense, were profoundly disturbed by present developments. Some forty M.P.s of left-wing politics invited me to meet them, and the *Manchester Guardian, Catholic Herald, New Statesman and Nation* as well as various papers in India, Australia and Germany made sympathetic references to my proposals for an enquiry.

The *Manchester Guardian* commented editorially that: "If any of the possible developments of modern weapons were to emerge, the alternative of non-violent resistance might be as Sir Stephen suggests, the best means to defend our way of life."

The Bishop of Manchester raised the matter in the Lords and other churchmen backed the idea. It was a policy, wrote the Editor of the *Catholic Herald*, which he had no doubt "would receive the blessing of the Holy See and the great religious leaders of the world".

I also discovered in the course of "off the record" talks that the proposal was being taken seriously by several eminent serving officers. This did not surprise me since top-level service people are often much more flexibly minded about defence questions than are their political masters, who correctly reflect the ignorance and traditionally conservative attitude of mind towards defence problems of most of the electorate.

Although public support for my suggestion that an enquiry would be worth-while came in the first instance chiefly from the political left, I received a number of letters from a more generally representative section of the population and a study of the correspondence suggested that there are thousands of people who are profoundly disturbed and worried about the present state of affairs and eagerly looking for a solution to our defence problems which *might* provide us with an escape from perplexing and alarming dilemmas.

Although it was easy enough to outline my general idea, I was conscious that my own mind was by no means clear about the nature of the many novel problems which would be created if the U.K. decided to adopt the alternative basis for its defence policy.

To take refuge in the statement that it was precisely in order to ascertain what these problems would be that I was asking for an enquiry was evasive action and not very courageous. I decided it was my duty to make an attempt to enlarge and elaborate the outline of the idea published in the news-letter in order to stimulate discussion and try to find out whether there was a *prima facie* case for a large-scale enquiry. This book is a personal contribution to the debate and claims to be no more than that.

The reader may be surprised to notice that it begins with a chapter on the nature of war.

This is relevant to the theme of the book for the following reasons:

Since about 1930 I have experienced growing doubts as to whether our defence arrangements were based on a sound understanding of the nature of war and (without anticipating here the contents of Chapter I) my conclusion, strongly reinforced by events from 1936-57, is that in the strategy of Total War there has been a deplorable neglect of the importance of political warfare and much over-emphasis on the significance of military operations. This will be an old story to those who have read my news-letter for the past twenty years and recall—for example—a private attempt to conduct political warfare against the Nazis in 1939 which, relative to the small scale of its operations, was extremely successful.

The development of nuclear weapons on the side of military force has only added extreme urgency to the need to solve a defence problem which was becoming increasingly tiresome at the end of the pre-nuclear age. Even with so-called conventional weapons the destructive capacity of military operations seemed to be approaching a state of affairs in which military victory was only obtainable at a price (in which had to be included the economic cost of preparation for defence) so great that it was becoming unreasonable.

The nuclear weapon may be the last straw which will break the camel's back and therefore its significance is that it seems to oblige us to look into the whole question of the anatomy of the already overloaded military camel and see whether he has served his purpose and should be replaced by some other animal.

That is why we must start with a probe into the nature of war which is that form of relationship between sovereign states which has caused us to load up the camel with his expensive, heavy, conventional burden and now demands that he shall also support a radio-active nuclear surcharge!

PART ONE

CHAPTER ONE

THE NATURE OF WAR

WAR IS A WORD used to describe a relationship between sovereign states. To most people the word WAR means some form of military activity. If armed forces are operating, the nation is "at war"; if they are not, "we are at peace". Of course "most people" are fully entitled to attach to any word whatever meaning they choose but they should know (which they do not) that in co-relating war with military operations they are giving to this word a much narrower meaning than its origins entitle it to claim.

Further reflection may lead "most people" to suspect that they have been deceiving themselves in saying that war means simply military operations and that if no bangs are taking place we are at peace; for in order to discuss the various kinds of non-peaceful relations between sovereign states they have had to invent qualifying phrases such as *total* war; *political* war; *cold* war; *economic* war; *nuclear* war and—for example—the phrase "the cold war" has come into existence because it was only too evident, especially in the example of the relationship between the Soviet Union and the West during the period after World War II, that although the Soviet Union and the U.K. were bound together by a treaty of twenty years' duration, there was no peace between them even though their military forces were not fighting each other.

Indeed so unpeaceful were relations, that the rulers of the Soviet Union (who had taken to heart the teachings of the genius Lenin who thoroughly understood the true nature of war) were often on record as stating in the clearest possible manner that they were actively engaged in the task of spreading Communism and therefore destroying the free way of life.[1]

[1] As recently as 2nd June, 1957, Mr. Khrushchev said: "With regard to the ideology of capitalist and socialist countries, we have never concealed that there will be a struggle in this field, an ideological struggle. . . . I once said that if an atomic war came it would be capitalism that would perish in that war. This I repeat today. But we think that capitalism should be destroyed . . . through an ideological and economic struggle."

Because there has been, and still is, a great deal of misunderstanding about the *nature* of war, this has led to error about the *object* of war.

During the first half of this century war has become Total. In its military manifestations it has become an activity absorbing the whole of the resources of the nation and a faulty appreciation of the purpose of such a formidable and all-embracing national effort is a very serious matter. A nation can stand a reasonable number of national mistakes such as the Ground Nuts Scheme in East Africa, but to make a mistake about the object of a major war may be catastrophic.

The word War is derived from an old English word WERRE and an old Northern French word of the same spelling from which is derived the modern *guerre*. The word WERRE came from the old High German WERRA which meant confusion, discord or strife and was derived—so it is assumed—from the Teutonic roots *werz* and *wers*, whence we also get the modern word "worse".

I have been told that it is unlikely that the tribes who used the word *werre* some 1,500 years ago had a word specifically intended to mean what we should now call military operations and nothing else. In their relatively primitive societies, in which the largest unit was the tribe, a state of discord or strife between tribes would normally be equated with violent action and diplomatic contacts would be unusual. War in those days must have been total and a Saxon raid on England would not always be preceded by an ultimatum! Then came a period during which a practice grew up for states to have professional armed forces trained and maintained exclusively for the use of violence in the form of military operations.

This development reached its climax at the beginning of the nineteenth century. Then came the conscript armies and with the twentieth century we swing rapidly back to the conception of the nation in arms, or Total War.

It is important to recognize that the root idea expressed by *werre* was the general notion of strife.

Since men's actions and ideas are related as is the thunder to the lightning, every action is the child of an idea.[1] Therefore

---

[1] Children and ill-informed adults are more frightened of the thunder than of the lightning. It is the lightning (the idea) which is significant.

strife or discord *must* be the product of a mental process, of a difference in ideas or opinion, whether the strife exists between two persons, two groups within a nation, two nations or two groups of nations.

Therefore the fundamental meaning of WAR is that it is the expression of a difference of opinion. The object of war must therefore be defined as follows: THE OBJECT OF WAR IS TO CHANGE THE ENEMY'S MIND. This simple and almost platudinous statement is of supreme importance and a failure to remember it and to use it as a guide to national strategy has led to the most deplorable results.

Confining our attention solely to events since 1914 the key statement mentioned above has never been given its true and fundamental importance. Professionals have often described the object of war as being that of: "*Imposing* our will upon the enemy." This is too narrow a definition. Imposition is only one way—and not necessarily the best way of bringing the enemy's thinking into harmony with ours.

II

I will consider how this statement about the object of war stands up to the test of what happened in the two world wars. At the beginning of each world war the issue between the British and German governments was reasonably clear and it was a difference of opinion of an ideological character.

The outbreak of military operations had been preceded by a state of tension between the two states and—as we shall see in the next chapter—this tension was less clearly moral or ideological before World War I than before World War II.

In 1912 as in 1937 there was a state of *werre* or conflict between the U.K. and Germany and it was reflected in an armaments race. Both sides were convinced that if the tension continued and became more actute the situation might develop into a trial of physical strength. In the years before World War I the British nation was divided in its opinion as to whether the Germany of the Kaiser William II was making reasonable claims for a place in the sun (the have-nots asking the haves for something) or whether Germany was a ruthless militaristic nation prepared to act without any regard for the rights of others or accepted principles of international law and the peaceful settlement of disputes.

It was *the act* of the German invasion of Belgium which rallied the mass of the British people behind their Government and convinced them that Germany had thus revealed the truly immoral nature of her policy.

In the years immediately preceding World War II, the ruthless policies and brutalities of the Nazi régime, to which Mussolini's Fascism had provided a pale introduction, had already created a state of acute ideological conflict between Great Britain (and other democratic powers) and the German Reich. Although the phrase had not yet been forced into existence, there was a state of tension we should now call a cold war. Vaguely in many men's minds in Britain, but conspicuously *not* in the minds of the Cabinet if their actions and speeches correctly reflected their thoughts, the idea began to grow that in Nazism we were confronted with evil ideas.

In 1939 Hitler's assault on Poland, which followed so close on the heels of his rape of Czechoslovakia, was an act that once again roused the British people to action in defence of law and against the unrestricted exercise of national sovereignty. In each case there were all kinds of subsidiary reasons which caused the men in charge of Britain's affairs to decide that violence must be used to curb violence. But, unless it be argued that it is less creditable to do the right thing—or what people believe to be the right thing—because to do so is also advantageous, I believe it to be true that in 1914 and in 1939 considerations of expediency were secondary in importance in the minds of the electorate when the man in the pub and the woman at the sink made up their minds "that this sort of thing will not do; we must act".

As I have remarked above, each world war was launched from a predominantly moral slipway and reflected a discord, strife or dispute about ideas, about conceptions of what was *right* and what was *wrong*. The British Prime Minister in his Guildhall speech on the 9th November, 1914 outlined our war aims: "We shall never sheathe the sword which we have not lightly drawn . . . until the rights of the smaller nationalities of Europe are placed upon an unassailable foundation and until the military domination of Prussia is wholly and finally destroyed."

THE NATURE OF WAR

Later on Mr. Lloyd George described the purpose of the War as being "the war to end wars". And the German Chancellor von Bethmann-Hollweg—unlike Hitler—felt it to be necessary, partly no doubt to satisfy German opinion, to excuse the invasion of Belgium by the plea of "military necessity."

In his broadcast on 3rd September, 1939 the British Prime Minister said: "It is the evil things that we shall be fighting against—brute force, bad faith, injustice, oppression and persecution—and against them I am certain that the right will prevail." He also said: "In this war we are not fighting against you, the German people, for whom we have no bitter feelings, but against a tyranny and foresworn régime, which has betrayed not only you, its own people, but the whole of western civilization and all that you and we hold dear." Both Asquith's speech in 1914 and Chamberlain's broadcast in 1939 accurately expressed the national reason for the war. If this was not so then the two Prime Ministers were expressing humbug on a national scale.

The author of this book was invited by the B.B.C. to give the first general broadcast talk after the outbreak of war when normal programmes were resumed. Asked for my opinion as to the subject I said: "There can only be one subject and it must be 'Why we are at war '." This being agreed (and time was in short supply) I retired to a room in Broadcasting House and drafted the talk. Some key sentences were:

"The fundamental reason why we are at war, why we are going to win this war, why in the widest sense we cannot lose the war, is because we are defending certain things which are far more lasting than frontier boundaries, individual lives or economic considerations . . . we are at war because France, Great Britain and the Dominions . . . stand in the world for an interpretation of life which is sometimes called democratic. . . . We are at war to defend moral values . . . it is a crusade upon which we are engaged and we must be for ever on guard lest in the heat of battle and passion of war, we lose sight even momentarily of the principles for which we are now preparing to make every sacrifice within our power."[1]

The head of the Talks Department—an ex-Indian civil servant from the North-West Frontier of India—was amazed

[1] The full text is in *The Listener*, 10th September, 1939.

when he read the script. "Do you really believe this is why we are at war?" "I do," was my reply, "and if I did not, I would oppose the war. Why do *you* think we are at war?" His reply was: "We are at war to beat the Huns."

This was early evidence of a confusion of thought as to war aims which, in 1939 (as in 1914), soon spread to all sections of the community.

It will be within the recollections of those of my readers who lived through World War I that in the struggle the issues became more and more confused as moral principles were sacrificed to military requirements. Secret treaties, contradictory promises to secure allies and so forth emerged like skeletons at the feast of the victors at Versailles and, notwithstanding the desperate efforts of the idealist, President Wilson, turned that gathering into one of the most prolonged and in some respects discreditable international trading markets of history. The goods being traded were the futures of millions of human beings.

In World War II a similar blurring over of the initial purposes of the war can be observed from a study of various statements. Many of them are reproduced in a book I wrote during the war.[1] These statements only cover the period 1939-41 and the coping stone on the structure which buried deep Mr. Chamberlain's statement of 3rd September, 1939 was the announcement on 15th January, 1943 that the object of the war was the "unconditional surrender" of the German nation.[2] Eighteen months earlier on 14th August, 1941 the eight point declaration of the Atlantic Charter had been issued by the U.S.A. and Great Britain. Point number eight has a particular and prophetic interest in connection with the question being discussed in this book. Its wording is as follows:

"They (the President of the U.S.A. and Prime Minister of the U.K.) believe that all of the nations of the world, for realistic as well as spiritual reasons, must come to the abandonment of the use of force. . . ."

[1] *Total Victory* by Stephen King-Hall (Faber & Faber): see pages 124-44.
[2] Cooked up almost by accident by Roosevelt and Churchill at Casablanca the basic purpose of this militarily foolish document was the product of a statement which would satisfy Stalin, then suspected of toying with the idea of reverting to his 1939-40 policy of co-operating with Hitler.

III

A state of war (*werre*) is the consequence of a conflict of ideas between the governments of sovereign states and this ideological tension must exist—usually for a considerable period of time—before one side decides that it will resort to violence to enforce its will on the other nation. This resort to violence is regarded chiefly as a process of imposing ideas upon the enemy rather than a means of converting him to accepting ideas.

"Diplomatic relations" which is a phrase used to describe the discussion and argument phase of a war are (at any rate theoretically) broken off as soon as violence begins.[1]

When the British Prime Minister declared on that historic Sunday morning of 3rd September, 1939 that: "it is the evil things that we shall be fighting against", he was not announcing a discovery he had made the night before. The "evil things" had been in full display for several years. Yet it was not until it was decided that armed force must be used—and an ultimatum to this effect sent to Hitler—that officially the fight began!

Up till midnight on the 2nd we were not *at War* with Hitler, we were *at Peace*! An absurd and striking example of the stupidity of thinking that war only means military operations.

The historian will look in vain in the records of events from, say, 1936-39 for much evidence that it was—as it should have been—the determined policy of His Majesty's Government to combat Nazi ideology and "change the minds" of the German people without whose moral support Hitler could not have existed for a week. Yet within a few hours of the end of a period (1936-39), during which the British Government had never shown the slightest indication of getting to work on

[1] In 1923, before the Chinese had picked up some bad habits from the West I helped to referee a local war in and around Amoy between three conflicting factions. With twenty-five British sailors I was in a small British concession 400 yards long and a 100 yards deep. It contained the offices of a British bank and the British Consulate and was a convenient centre at which representatives of the combatants could meet. They did so very frequently and I then learnt that, far from diplomatic relations being broken off, it was considered that simply because the situation had deteriorated into violence it was more necessary than ever to continue to negotiate!

The modern parallel to this sensible old-Chinese attitude can be seen in the summoning of special assemblies of the U.N. in times of grave crisis.

German minds, the British Prime Minister was assuring these Germans that we esteemed them so much that we would shed our blood to rescue them from Hitler! The extent to which we could have changed German minds between 1936-39 and what steps were needed to make the attempt is irrelevant. We never tried to do it notwithstanding the fact that Goebbels was spending millions annually in propaganda to fortify the German mind against a possible democratic attack—a clear indication (as I thought and wrote at the time) that its domestic public opinion was the Achilles' heel of the Nazi régime, as indeed it is of every dictatorship.

However, as War only starts (officially) with the first shot, it is—or it was as recently as 1939—idle to expect anything to be done to win the war by changing the enemy's mind before war degenerates into violence.

Thus was perpetrated the first and most expensive error consequent upon not understanding the true nature of war and its object. An error of omission.

Nevertheless, as we have seen at the outbreak of hostilities the ideological nature of each world war was implied and its object clearly described in the speeches and statements made by national leaders.

Yet the object—to bring the enemy round to our way of thinking—was soon lost sight of. Why was this? Why has it always been so and will be so until people can think clearly about War?

The reason is this: Once military operations begin the issues of life or death present themselves starkly to the individual. Kill or be killed. Death is the most dramatic and tremendous event in the life of a man; he has no anticipations or thoughts about his birth. A good murder story remains unchallenged as the most news-worthy event known to Fleet Street. Military operations are dramatic and exciting.

Up to 1914 there was glamour in violent war and civilians could read at their breakfast tables about the exploits of their professional armed forces secure in the knowledge that, short of military defeat, their contribution to the war was to be "business as usual" and more of it if possible. The 1914-18 violent war began to alter all that, as the flower of the nation perished in Flanders, Gallipoli, Mesopotamia and on the sea approaches to Britain. By the 1939-45 war the reality of violence came to the homeland and many a charwoman proceeding to her daily task in the office of a great city was on more active service than her son who was in the garrison at (say) Gibraltar.

But because the military operations in Total War are like an insatiable furnace which, in order to be kept at the highest possible temperature, must be fed with all the spiritual and material resources of the nation, the war (by about the third year) and everything to do with it becomes almost indistinguishable from the needs of everyday life. "Is your journey really necessary?" . . . "Save for shells." War becomes the life of the nation and the purpose of the life of the nation is to wage War. Liberties and freedoms are curtailed and even in Britain the executive at certain moments in World War II exercised the powers it had been granted by Parliament to an extent which sailed pretty close to the wind of dictatorship. The citizen is immersed from morning to night in a flood of propaganda designed to achieve the single purpose of "winning the war" which naturally enough appears to be, and to a limited extent is, the achievement of military victory.

Military Victory and then the Victory celebrations—those were the ultimate objectives for most people whilst the ghastly casualties were darkening their lives in World War I and the bombs and V1's and V2's were falling in World War II.

The people at the top are well aware that one day there will be a cease fire and that this will not be the end of what they call "the war". But one cannot blame them for feeling that the less said about this the better as otherwise people's minds would be distracted from the job in hand, which is military victory.

"The art of governing men," said Clemenceau, "is infinitely more complex than that of massacring them."

However comprehensive they may be, military operations and subsidiary activities such as political warfare, special service operations, economic warfare, etc., are only means to the end of Total Victory.

Why *Total* Victory?

The word victory as usually understood and used means in effect military victory and this, if viewed in sober historical perspective, *can* be too complete and an actual hindrance to the achievement of Total Victory.

What is meant by Total Victory? It means a settlement which is a real peace because both sides regard its terms as beneficial and to be supported. Bearing in mind that I have described war as essentially a conflict of ideas, the state of war can only be ended and transformed into a state of peace when there is no longer a conflict of ideas and when a settlement is reached which embodies agreed ideas. This is Total Victory and genuine Peace. For example: The Treaty of Versailles was the reflection of a military victory. People on the allied side were disposed to say that this result will show the Germans that might is *not* right. It did nothing of the sort. The terms were *imposed* upon the Germans, therefore the thought in the minds of many of them must have been that (irrespective as to whether might was right or wrong) Germany's mistake was in not having had enough might, otherwise Lloyd George and Clemenceau would have been sitting in the dock!

Towards the end of his life Earl Lloyd George told me that he had come to the conclusion that an agreed settlement between the Allies and Germany, which might have been achieved through the Lansdowne proposals in 1917, would have been a wise move. I think he was right.

If war is fundamentally a conflict of ideas, which may in certain circumstances lead to the use of violence in the shape of military operations, and if a Total Victory is a state of affairs in which there is no longer a conflict of ideas but agreement, then there is real Peace and not an armistice.

IV

If the object of war is to change the enemy's mind, the art of defence must be to bring about this change as expeditiously and economically as possible.

It is an axiom that the best method of defence is the attack and I shall have more to say about this at a later stage when we come to the particular defence problems of the U.K. at this time (1957).

Let us in the meanwhile consider what are the ways and means open to a government at war (difference of opinion with another government) to change the enemy's mind?

They fall into two and possibly three categories.

First: Methods which aim at bringing physical pressure to bear on the body so that its brain says: "To avoid further misery I will give in and concede to the victor what he demands." In practice this is the purpose of military operations, which are designed to change the enemy's mind by making him suffer. I call this the Battle of the Bodies.

Second: Methods which aim at persuading the enemy that one's ideas are better than his. This is an operation designed to convert the enemy. It is an appeal to his reason. I call this the Battle of the Brains.

The third category into which mind-changing operations can be classified is a recent arrival on the stage of war. It consists of what is commonly called brain-washing. I am not sure how important from the point of view of the purpose of this study the technique may be but an enquiry might clear up the point. I am disposed to think that the technique is a kind of cross between the Battle of the Bodies and the Battle of the Brains. It is not easy to detect where political warfare of a relatively honest character ends and brain-washing begins. There is no doubt that when the victim is an individual the extreme forms of brain-washing are in truth violent assaults on the brain comparable to blows on the body. But there is also mass brain-washing exemplified in a relatively harmless form by modern advertising and less agreeably in communist indoctrination.[1] I am bound to record that after witnessing the rehabilitation techniques used on Mau Mau adherents in Kenya I was left with many uncertainties to which only time will provide an answer.

The question to be considered is what are the relative advantages and disadvantages of the two main methods of obtaining Total Victory by changing the enemy's mind so that the settlement reached expresses a common point of view? An agreement reached by consent is likely to be more permanent and stable than one based on the triumph of violence and history is littered with examples of defeated nations nurturing feelings of revenge and planning to renew the struggle under more favourable conditions to themselves.

[1] The failure of this to produce results amongst the younger generation in Hungary is very significant (see Chapter II).

Furthermore a victory in the Battle of the Brains can be achieved before the Battle of the Bodies begins and this will save enormous expense and misery and avoid the almost inescapable danger that the Battle of the Bodies will become an end instead of a means.

The ideological nature of war is not changed if the struggle degenerates into military operations any more than the existence of the sun is affected by the presence of a fog which obscures its rays. This is true even if violence leads to a complete military victory for one of the belligerents. It is however an error to suppose that because military operations do not change the nature of war (but only its conduct) they are irrelevant to the solution of the problem of changing the enemy's mind. They can make an important and sometimes an essential contribution.

Before developing this point I must make it clear that for reasons we shall come to later on there are certain degrees of force which, because of their extreme violence, must be excluded from the considerations set forth below.

In the first place an obvious determination (reflected in the existence of armed forces) to resist aggression may cause the potential aggressor to change his mind; so can successful resistance. Whether or not the American colonies could have obtained their independence, or so much of it as they then wanted, without resorting to arms is a speculative question, but that by defeating the British forces in North America they created a climate of opinion in Britain which caused the British Government to abandon the struggle, is an historical fact. In Ireland and in Palestine *terrorism* (by London's definition) or *patriotic struggle* (in Dublin or Tel Aviv language) played a large part in changing the minds of British statesmen.

It should also be observed that a military victory does not of itself compel the victors to impose a settlement on the vanquished which leaves unresolved the basic conflict of ideas which are at the root of the war. A military victory can and indeed should enable the victors to so treat the vanquished that they (the vanquished) concede victory in the Battle of the Brains.

An example of this category was the Boer War 1899-1902. There was a difference of ideas between the British Government

and the Governments of the two Dutch Republics, which
degenerated into a situation in which the British determined to
enforce their ideas on the Boers. The immediate political object
of the war then became the extinction of the independence of
these two small sovereign states. After an unexpectedly lengthy
campaign military victory was achieved. Within a few years
there was a change of government in London and the two
Republics were given back their independence within the framework of Dominion status. This settlement was fully supported by
the majority of Boer leaders who had fought in the war and
led to the Union backing the United Kingdom in World Wars
I and II. In this case the military victory was used by the
victors to achieve a Total Victory by agreeing to a settlement
which was the reverse of what the military victory had been
designed to achieve.

The fact that to-day, fifty years later, this achievement and
settlement between Europeans in S. Africa is no longer ac-
claimed as the end of the story by Nationalist leaders in South
Africa does not detract from the value of fifty years of peace.

The situation at present (1957) in S. Africa, and in a less
acute form in parts of Central Africa, in the racial struggle
provides an interesting example illustrative of the truth that
one must not think of war only in terms of military conflict.

In the Union of S. Africa, as I observed the situation early
in 1957, it was clear that a "war" or conflict of ideas was raging
between the S. African Nationalist Government and the
emerging leaders of the Bantu people.

The policy and practice of *Apartheid* is a clear cut ideological
issue. All the armed force is on the side of the Nationalists. Yet
many European S. Africans are apprehensive that the struggle
may degenerate into violence (of the Mau Mau type) if the
tension increases.

Since the policy of *Apartheid* is economically absurd and
politically and morally in flat contradiction to the anti-racial
developments taking place all over the world it is almost
inconceivable that the Nationalists will succeed (not that they
are trying very hard) to change the Bantu mind and get
the Bantus to accept *Apartheid*. The Bantu leaders and their
European sympathizers are on the other hand endeavouring to
win the war by changing the Nationalist mind and the weapons

B

they are using are economic pressures (boycotts, etc.) and the mobilization of world public opinion. If the Union of South Africa is to avoid a blood bath it seems likely that the Nationalists will have to change their minds about *Apartheid*. The most that force can do is to postpone the day of reckoning.

The factor of world public opinion is an element of increasing importance in War. In the Boer War, to which reference has been made, a study of the Press and Parliamentary debates of that period show that civilized Western opinion was almost unanimously hostile to British policy which, in Western Europe, was regarded as an outstanding example of Imperialism in its most unworthy form and a natural sequel to the scandalous Jameson Raid. But the same sources of information show that the Conservative Government of those days treated this barrage of abuse and criticism from abroad with a lofty contempt. Much has changed in fifty years in this respect; a new factor has entered into the calculations of the political war-operator who is planning his campaign to change the enemy's mind. He has to reckon with the fact that force, if it is to be used, will be more effective if it can be clothed in the garments of international authority. He must consider how to use the Security Council and Assembly of the United Nations. This body is much criticized by those who misapprehend its purpose and expect it to be better than the nations which compose it, but the plain and indisputable fact remains that the most powerful states (and particularly of course the weaker ones) attach an immense amount of importance to making a good case at the U.N. A favourable vote at the U.N., even if when given in the Security Council it obliges the enemy to exercise the veto, is an asset not to be despised and of great value in an international dispute; i.e. a war or *werre*. It is particularly valuable to have the moral force implied in a majority backing at the U.N. if a state decides that the dispute should pass from the political to the military phase. The Korean War was a case in point. Nasser also owes a lot to the U.N.!

It must also be said that a complete military victory does not make it easy for the government of the victorious state to make a peace treaty likely to be reasonably acceptable to the vanquished. Passions and hatreds have been aroused, and deliberately so, on both sides, and statesmen (as at Paris in

1919) find themselves obliged by the pressure of popular
opinion to advocate measures they know to be impracticable
and unlikely to buttress Peace, e.g. "Hang the Kaiser".

The strategy of Total War demands the dove-tailing into a
common effort of political *and* military activities; an extremely
difficult exercise in the art of mixing oil and steam!—especially
since, as mentioned earlier in this chapter, once military
operations have started their fundamental purpose is forgotten
and those in charge of political warfare operations, as was
shown in both world wars, can never have their strategy and
tactics on a firm foundation of war aims. The political warfare
command then finds itself operating as a kind of subsidiary
department of the military command and asked so to organize
its propaganda that specific military operations will be more
successful, or that some neutral country will add its military
resources to the struggle.

The clash of ideas (i.e. the war)[1] between the democracies
and the Soviet Union is a most interesting and instructive
example of how the military aspects of war can confuse and
obscure its ideological content. When the strife between the
Nazis and the democracies degenerated into violence in 1939
Stalin soon revealed which side he was on or thought it wise
to be on. He gave the Nazis material aid and Molotov publicly
attacked British and French imperialist aggression. When
Hitler treacherously attacked his quasi-ally the British Prime
Minister went to the microphone and told the nation that
Russia was now our ally. This was perfectly correct and tactically proper within the context of military operations but, as
events have shown, it made no difference whatsoever to the
fundamental difference of ideas (or war) between the democracies and the Communists.

The persistence of this fundamental strife was revealed
(although the fact was not known to most of the British public)
by the unco-operative behaviour of the Soviet Union even
whilst we were military allies. To Stalin the alliance was a
mere tactical operation of limited and temporary value to be
discarded at the appropriate moment when the main struggle
between Communism and democracy could be resumed.

---

[1] This war which began in 1917 and after many changes in appearance took on
a new aspect in 1945-46 is usually called the Cold War.

The British people, convinced that War meant military operations and nothing else, were genuinely confused when they began to discover from Yalta onwards that our relations with "our brothers in arms, our gallant Russian allies" were not at all peaceful but increasingly tense! It seemed incredible, but Russian actions were so obviously menacing that the phrase "the cold war" came into circulation and eventually Nato was born. The Nato Treaty, be it noted, was (Article II excepted) an organization of military force. It reflected the conviction so widely held in the West that, if we were not *at peace*, the *only* contingency which had to be taken care of was an attack by armed force. There was certainly some truth in this, but it was not the whole truth. With one important exception the West took no action to plan a long-term political strategy to deal with the ideological and fundamental struggle with the Communists. The exception was Marshall Aid, which produced massive economic assistance for Western Europe and thus countered the danger that the Communist parties in the West, who were the spearheads of the Soviet offensive, would be able to seize power through the existence of widespread unemployment and social misery.

I have endeavoured in this chapter to take a new look at the nature of war, and for the following reason:

Our defence arrangements, which cost us approximately £1,500,000,000 per annum, are thought of and related to the use of armed force. The maintenance of this force, and if necessary its use, is described as preparation for war (for the safeguarding of peace) or for war if military operations begin. It is my contention, and has been for a number of years, that this mental co-relation of the word war with military force to the virtual exclusion—certainly up to 1946—of any other consideration has led to thinking about our defence problems in too narrow a framework.

This criticism is not quite so valid to-day as it was ten years ago because during the last decade it has been possible to detect the beginnings of an understanding that war between sovereign states comprehends more than the clash of armed force, but the gleam of light which has begun to flicker intermittently in the gloom which has enveloped thinking about the nature of war is not yet very impressive.

The existence of some germs of new thinking in the highest quarters about war is reflected in certain passages in the White Paper on Defence 1957 of which the following are examples (the italics are mine):

". . . the time has come to revise not merely the size *but the whole character of the defence plan.* The Communist threat remains, *but its nature has changed*" (para 3).

and:

". . . the overriding consideration in *all military planning* must be to prevent war rather than to prepare for it" (para 13).

I find it hard to understand what this means, but it seems to indicate a mental shift of some kind from conventional thinking about war.

We are not told in what respect the nature of the Communist threat has changed. I would welcome enlightenment on this discovery. But the above could be read as meaning that pre-military operation activities are to be given priority. If this interpretation is correct then the importance of the Battle of the Brains is beginning to be recognized at Cabinet level.

On the other hand there is plenty of evidence in the White Paper that Defence and War are still thought of almost exclusively in terms of armed force. For example:

". . . the *only* existing safeguard against major aggression is the power to *threaten* retaliation with nuclear weapons" (para 14).

or

". . . the frontiers of the free world, particularly in Europe, must be firmly defended on the ground. For *only* in this way can it be made clear that aggression will be resisted" (para 20).

Yet, as mentioned at the beginning of this chapter, if we do not understand or have too restricted an appreciation of the meaning of war and design our defence arrangements solely in terms of one aspect of war, we are led into grievous error.

In summary the conclusions the reader is asked to consider are as follows:

(a) War is a relationship between sovereign states.

(b) This particular relationship is caused by a difference of opinion or conflict of ideas.

(c) The *object* of war is to change the enemy's mind.

(d) There are several ways of changing men's minds.

(e) The two most important are by the power of reason (conversion) and the power of fear (military operations and other violent methods directed against enemy bodies). These two methods are respectively the Battle of the Brains and the Battle of the Bodies.

(f) The changing of a mind by reason is to be preferred to a change by fear but fear may have a beneficial role if intelligently used.

(g) Insufficient importance has hitherto been attached to political warfare both before and during military operations.

CHAPTER TWO

THE OBJECT OF DEFENCE

THE DIRECT COST of defence for the year 1956-57 was estimated at £1,483,000,000. This figure, in the region of 10 per cent of the gross national product, compares with estimates, subsequently reduced, of an average of £1,600,000,000 per annum for the period 1950-53. Figures of this size have been judged to be more than the economy of the country can stand. The Government rightly insists that part of the defence potential of the nation is a healthy economy and, from the strictly economic point of view, direct defence expenditure is an unproductive activity only justified on the grounds that it is a premium for an insurance policy against the contingency of war.[1]

Much of the expenditure on defence is normally devoted to the manufacture of potential "free exports". These are explosions to be delivered free of charge on enemy territory. Experience shows that a great deal of the destruction they cause will ultimately be restored at the expense of the exporter —provided he "wins the war".

Apart from the direct expenditure shown in the estimates, there is a very large indirect expenditure represented by the loss of wealth which would have been available for non-military purposes if all the labour and material absorbed by an armaments programme and the maintenance of armed forces with their establishments were not so used. Some 7 per cent of the working population of the U.K. in 1957 were either in the Services or supporting them. One-eighth of the output of the metal-using industries was devoted to defence. What is the purpose of this formidable effort?

We are trying to defend something against a potential aggressor. *But what are we trying to defend and against whom and*

[1] In his famous book *The Great Illusion*, Sir Norman Angell pointed out that in modern conditions it was an error to suppose that war could be a worthwhile economic enterprise. The story of German reparations after World War I proved his wisdom.

against what sort of aggression are we defending IT? This is a deep question and clichés such as "Queen and Country" do not get us far below the surface. But it is a question which should not be evaded and to which we must find an answer in order to judge whether this great defence effort in the military sphere is the right kind of defence policy and whether there is enough of it.

It seems reasonable to assume that what we are trying to defend must be something closely associated with the polity, i.e. the whole social organization and mode of government of the nation, and there are two parts which make up the whole of what we mean when we speak of the British Nation (U.K.).

There are the visible and outward manifestations of the nation such as the 50 million people, their towns and factories, ports and mines; in short the physical assets of Great Britain. That is one part of the nation. The other part is the national way of life, which has emerged from the historical evolution of the nation. This way of life is expressed in practices which in their turn need certain institutions for their proper functioning. The existence of the mechanisms of the institution does not guarantee the proper functioning of the institution. The practice of a free press requires newspapers, but the existence of newspapers does not ensure a free press.

The most important of all the institutions which exist to express the British way of life is Parliament.

What we are trying to defend is a combination of the material and the spiritual; of physical goods and properties and ideas which, for their full expression, require the free functioning of various institutions. This statement leads to certain questions.

What part, if any, of the various factors which make up our way of life should be regarded as more vital than any other? Looking back over our history during the past few hundred years, has the object of our defence changed in its emphasis? As regards the first question my answer is given in the next chapter which is devoted to an analysis of our way of life and, for reasons set forth in that chapter, the conclusion is that it is an IDEA, that of the freedom of the individual, which is the basic foundation and most significant feature of our way of life.

The second question is best approached by considering the nature of our foreign policy, because this policy and defence policy are opposite sides of the same medal.

Although it is impossible in the space available to deal at any length with the evolution of British foreign policy over the centuries, enough can be outlined to provide reasons for supposing that it has altered substantially *in character*.

When men are organized into a tribal system the warriors are expected to be able to defend the material property of the tribe; the land, the cattle, the women.

Wars between tribes are conflicts of ideas about who should own wealth; the purpose of defence is to safeguard property. Another relatively simple purpose of defence is the case in which it is intended to safeguard the personal authority of a ruler or his dynasty.

It is unlikely that at the Battle of Hastings the English archers had any advanced ideas about freedom and democracy. They lived in a feudal system and their man was Harold. The Normans also lived in a feudal system and their man was William. The Norman barons were interested in conquering England, not in order to introduce social reforms or spread French culture amongst the inhabitants of this island, but in order to acquire real estate. The English nobility fought to hold what they had and no doubt appealed (so far as any appeal was necessary) to their followers to aid them in repelling the Norman bandits, who must have been regarded as the latest and most formidable examples of a long succession of continental would-be conquerors of Great Britain.

History moved on and the European peoples began to crystallize into national states. The Renaissance led to the sea-voyages and explorations and the wars of the sixteenth–eighteenth centuries were basically caused by differences of opinion as to which nation—the Spanish, the Dutch, the French or the British—should have the major share of influence and commercial monopoly in Asia and America. In making this simplification it has not been forgotten that dynastic and religious considerations also came into the picture.

These were the empire-building wars and their principal purpose was material gain. They were acquisitive wars.

At that time the principal medium of communication from one part of the globe to another was the surface of the sea, so military victory depended upon sea-power and this was the cause of the final triumph of Great Britain when Napoleon was caged on St. Helena. During this period the British were engaged in a war with the people of their N. American colonies and, although material considerations were certainly well to the fore in the minds of the British Cabinet, the war had a strong ideological content in the thoughts of the Americans, whose case was supported by the Opposition in the British Parliament.

Having established their world supremacy—except for the misfortune, so it then seemed, of the loss of the American colonies—the British during the nineteenth century embarked on operations designed to extend the Colonial Empire. But, though Governments believed that to extend the Colonial Empire was desirable as a means of adding to the military[1] and economic strength of the mother country, there was also a feeling that it was Britain's destiny to spread the Christian gospel and good (i.e. democratic) government. This was the White Man's Burden and there were considerable differences of opinion amongst white men of various nationalities as to which group should bear the heaviest burden. This was particularly noticeable in Africa where France, Germany and Britain were "at war" with each other about their respective shares of Africa. These African "wars", which reached a degree of considerable tension in the 1890's, never degenerated into military operations between the great powers but it was a very near thing between France and Great Britain when the Fashoda incident occurred on the Upper Nile in 1898. The Agadir incident in Morocco in 1911 between Germany on the one hand and France and Britain on the other was another of many incidents of the war for colonies and spheres of influence in Africa.

A comparable process took place in Asia, where China was assumed to be in a state of disintegration. In this part of the world the competing European powers were faced with a non-white competitor in the shape of Japan. When the latter defeated Imperial China at the end of the nineteenth century the European powers led by Russia combined to prevent the Japanese from garnering the full fruits of victory. This caused the Japanese to plan for their successful war against Russia in 1904-5. It is interesting to note that the U.S.A., which had begun to become interested in Far Eastern affairs, was already

---

[1] Especially through the creation of a powerful Indian Army.

taking up an ideological and moral attitude towards European and Japanese designs on China. The Americans (in those days) were disposed to regard themselves as the protectors of the Chinese against the wicked Europeans.

The Boer War, followed by the establishment of the Union of South Africa, marked a turning point in British foreign policy and hence in Britain's defence policy. It marked the end of imperial expansion by force and the beginning of a strictly defensive policy. The growing power of Germany and her demand for "a place in the sun" caused the British to regard their defence arrangements as being necessary to guard what they had got from German imperial ambitions. The British method of doing this was to conclude an entente cordiale (plus private staff talks) with the French, who were themselves allied with Tsarist Russia out of a common fear of the modern Germany which had been born of France's defeat in the 1870 war. The Germans were allied with Austro-Hungary and Italy.

This was the notion of the Balance of Power. The theory was that, provided the armed forces on each side were kept at about equal strength, it would be manifest that neither side could "win the war" and so there would be no war.

It was frequently pointed out that, as there was no superior supra-national authority acting as an umpire, each side was the judge of what it deemed to be necessary to have in order to produce a balance. The result of this state of affairs was bound to be—and history proved it to be so—an armaments race, with each side leap-frogging the other.[1]

This meant that there were bound to be periods during which one side was temporarily superior to the other and therefore tempted to attack.

Moreover, questions of national character, organizational ability, military skills and industrial capacity were all relevant to the national war potential and could not be accurately taken into account in endeavouring to decide whether or not a balance existed.

It is significant and perhaps rather ominous that in the language of 1957 the balance of power idea of 1900-14 (or

[1] A contemporary example of the practical difficulties of applying this policy in the absence of a supreme authority is the arms race between Israel and the Arab States.

earlier) could have been talked about as the *deterrent idea*! Since military victory was theoretically impossible in a conflict between equals they were supposedly "deterred" from making war.

In addition to reliance on the balance of power the British made great efforts to retain a margin of naval superiority over Germany; so our naval forces were concentrated in Home Waters. There were people who pointed out that the writing about the future of Britain's position in a world of power politics was beginning to be outlined on the wall of history for, whereas during the nineteenth century—the era of the Pax Britannica—a two-power or even a three-power standard of naval strength had been publicly stated as essential to the security of the British Empire on which the sun never set, now in the first decade of the twentieth century Britain was bargaining for a 1·6 to 1 standard of superiority over Germany.

After World War I the British were obliged to concede parity to the U.S.A. and in 1957 the famous British Navy, behind whose shelter the Americans had been able to make a reality of the Monroe doctrine and build up their great country in a peace only broken by their own civil war, is a very small affair compared to the naval forces of the U.S.A.

With wisdom which comes after the event it seems likely that as Britain's strength, relative to that of the U.S.A., Japan and Germany began to decline, her correct policy of defence should have been to work whole-heartedly for collective security and the establishment before 1914 of some kind of a League of Nations. Whatever may have been the advantages of the enforcement of British ideas and policies by allowing war (*werre*) to develop into violence during the period 1600-1900 there were, in 1900, overwhelmingly strong reasons why Britain should wish for peace. The maintenance of the *status quo* or, if that were impossible, its alteration as slowly and peacefully as possible was her manifest interest; the reverse consideration so far as the rate of change was concerned was Germany's interest and so interesting to her rulers that they were prepared, as 1914 showed, to endeavour to bring it about by force.

Some recognition of this British overriding interest is to be found in a speech made by Sir Edward Grey in the Commons on 13th March. 1911[1] in which he referred to the need for some form of collective security: "Some armies and navies would remain no doubt, . . . not in rivalry with each other, but as the police of the world . . . the great nations of the world are in bondage, in increasing bondage, at the present moment to their armies and navies . . . they may discover, as individuals have discovered, that law is a better remedy than force." President Taft of the U.S.A. had made some proposals which caused Sir Edward to make this speech. Nothing came of this American initiative.

It can be argued with much force that World War I was the first mainly moral war waged by the British people. It was a war which began to reflect the change which took place after the Boer War. *Autres temps autres mœurs.* No doubt our naval ancestors felt that Napoleon was a bad man. But I judge that they thought that the particular wickedness of the French (which was epitomized in the person of Napoleon) was their desire to take something away from the British. Ideas that the Napoleonic wars were ideological struggles between British conservatism, monarchy and Parliamentary government on the one hand, and French agnosticism, republicanism and left-wing revolutionary ideas on the other, soon faded away as Napoleon showed clearly that he was a Corsican turned into a French Imperialist.

When the assassination of the Austrian Archduke at Sarajevo precipitated a crisis which was to prove that the balance of power was not in equilibrium, it was, as I have pointed out on page 24, the German invasion of Belgium which brought Britain into the war. I am not pretending that considerations of power politics and the fear that a victorious Germany supreme on the Continent would be a menace to Britain[2] did not weigh heavily with the Cabinet, but there was also a moral feeling that the war was necessary to fight and defeat militarism and the doctrine that Might was Right.

It was a war for a principle, even if during its conduct and at the peace settlement the principles were largely forgotten. It was called: "the war to end war" and some of us believed this.

---

[1] *Hansard*, Vol. xxii, Col. 1988. The whole speech is well worth reading to-day (1957) and very apt to our present situation.

[2] Antwerp—the pistol pointed at the heart of England.

We were young. The creation of the League of Nations enshrined that principle.

In 1914 the U.K. Government declared war on behalf of themselves and the Dominions; the latter, sitting as sovereign states at Versailles, were not going to stand for that again and the Statute of Westminster was the result. The Commonwealth was born and Commonwealth military policy so far as it could be said to exist could only be defensive, it could not be acquisitive.

Another result of World War I was the emergence of Communist Russia with its anti-capitalist ideology. A half-hearted attempt by the allies to translate the conflict of ideas between themselves and the Bolsheviks into military operations failed and this violence strengthened the local standing of Lenin and his associates. The military operation conducted by the victorious allies against the Bolsheviks immediately after World War I provides an interesting example of the use of force not only failing to change the mind of the enemy but actually strengthening the ideological hold of the enemy government on its people.

The rise of Hitler and the totalitarian policies he introduced created a situation in which the difference of opinion (or war) between the British and the Germans (at least those who supported Hitler) was ideological. But just as some Germans resisted Hitler, whilst others supported him without realizing the implications of their action, so in Britain some people saw the true meaning of the Nazi danger whilst others believed he could be appeased and might become law-abiding.

The rape of Czechoslovakia and Munich opened the eyes of most of the British and the assault on Poland caused Britain to use force for reasons more comprehensively ideological than on any previous occasion in her history.

Some realization—but much too little—that this was so appeared from time to time during the war but, for reasons already described (see page 28) military considerations soon overshadowed all else.

There was, however, an interesting and significant difference in one respect between World Wars I and II and that was the small amount of hatred evinced by the British people and Press towards the German nation in World War II as compared with World War I.

Why was this? Why was it that during World War I it was impossible to play the music of German composers in London (though the Germans listened to British music and played Shakespeare in Berlin) and almost necessary for British people with German names to anglicize them? In World War I, the First Lord of the Admiralty was hounded from office because his name was Battenberg, and I saw a lady, anxious to avoid her dachshund from being stoned, fasten a small Union Jack to its tail before she took it for a walk! It will be within the knowledge of any middle-aged reader that this kind of hatred for everything German did not exist during World War II. German refugees were well treated and there was no rush to anglicize German names or ban Wagner from concert programmes. When visiting bombed-out families from Liverpool who had fled northwards to my constituency, I found that it made no appeal to them to be told that our bombers were destroying German cities. One woman, destitute and with a small family round her, said: "Why should I want some poor —— German woman to go through what I've been through?"

At the end of World War I there was a vociferous demand for the "hanging of the Kaiser" and for the Germans to be "squeezed until the pips squeaked". At the end of World War II there was little enthusiasm for the Nuremberg trials of war criminals although Goering and Co. were far more responsible for German policies, especially the slaughter of the Jews, than had been Kaiser Wilhelm II, who died at Doorn a well respected figure.

I suggest that the difference between the popular attitude in the U.K. towards Germans in World War I and World War II was due to a kind of vague and perhaps subconscious feeling that the Prime Minister had been talking sense in his broadcast (see page 25) and that common people in both countries were victims of forces beyond their control and were not enemies of each other.

Although outwardly and, as the war developed, in the speeches of the war leaders the struggle was depicted as a clash between the armed forces of the contestants, it is my personal impression that many people felt that World War II was "something rather different" in character from World War I, and I guess that a man of World War I felt that there was more

of a moral principle at stake in that struggle than would have
been recognized by a man of the Napoleonic wars.

Another indication of this changing attitude by the nation
towards the object of war is provided by the respect with which
conscientous objectors were treated in World War II compared
with earlier wars. Also, in this struggle there was a greater
degree of national political unity than in any previous war and
the basic cause of this was agreement on the *principle* that
democracy was battling with totalitarianism.

After the end of the war the course of events gradually made
it clear that it was the Soviet policy to promote by all possible
means the extension of Communism. The Communists had
long realized that it was often more appropriate in war to
subordinate military force to subversive ideas and their
technique in this respect was abundantly illustrated in the first
decade after World War II. It soon became common form
all over the world to talk about the cold war, meaning the
ideological struggle between the upholders respectively of the
democratic and Communist practices and principles.

Immediately after World War II the balance of physical
power between the two warring groups was as follows: The
free nations possessed, or were believed to possess, a monopoly
of nuclear weapons, whereas the Soviet Union possessed a great
superiority in conventional weapons.

The menace to the free world of the Soviet policy so alarmed
most of the nations on the freedom side of the iron curtain that
they joined together to create the North Atlantic Treaty Organization (1949). Its original purpose and plan was to create
conventional forces of such size (e.g. 90 divisions), that they
would be sufficiently strong to repel a conventional armed
attack by the Soviet Union and satellites on Western Europe.
This hope was never realized even though, in an endeavour to
re-enforce the Nato potential, the West Germans were welcomed back into the camp of free nations and pressed to
re-arm.

The cold war has, on the whole, been a political and economic struggle between the Communist Soviet Union and the
democratic nations. On several occasions the temperature of
this cold war nearly reached the point of boil when "the war"
(werre) degenerates into violence and on one occasion it did

reach this point. I refer to the Korean campaign. Before the
Korean War there was the interesting case of the blockade of
Berlin. When the Soviet leaders decided to endeavour to force
the Allies to leave Berlin by cutting off land communication
between the West and the city, the Western powers had to
decide whether to retaliate violently or non-violently. It is
common knowledge that one school of thought advocated
sending an armoured column down the road to Berlin and
seeing what happened. In the event a more subtle and fundamentally non-violent *riposte* was adopted, that of the famous
airlift. This placed on the Russians the responsibility for starting
up a war if they shot down the civil planes carrying out the
airlift. This baffled the enemy although one must recognize
that there may be much force in the argument that as,
at that time, the allies had the monopoly of the nuclear
weapon this was probably a powerful deterrent in the mind
of Stalin.

The Korean War was most clearly a war about ideas and
not about things. It may have been a landmark in history.
President Truman recognized that this was Communist aggression expressed in violence and he reacted immediately in—as
we shall see in a moment—the traditional spirit of American
policy. Thanks to the fortunate absence of the Soviet Union
from the Security Council, the Korean War became a U.N. war
and the British Commonwealth contributed its brigade.

Then came Suez which, unlike the Berlin and Korean
episodes, was not strictly speaking part of the cold war. The
Suez episode was an astonishing and almost mysterious throw-
back to the pre-Boer War policy and was so archaically out of
harmony with the developments of intelligent thought in
Britain since 1900 that its abject failure was a foregone conclusion.

The Suez episode also revealed that a great many people,
perhaps the majority of the nation, were living in a dream-
world and did not know that the Victorian era was in the
history books. Their voice was that of the lady who wrote:
"It was nice to hear the British Lion roar if only for a short
time." The Suez episode was of an educational value to the
nation comparable to that received by our ancestors at the
hands of the American colonists.

II

The British—whose changing values about what they have wished to defend I shall summarize in a moment—were not the only nation who evolved in this respect and a few words about American and French ideas of defence and foreign policy will not be out of place.

The French, bled white by World War I, then made a desperate and logical effort to transfer real power to the League of Nations and a businesslike scheme of collective security. Locarno and all that. In this matter the British were not helpful. They were not as weak as the French, they still held India and the Indian Army, they were supreme in the Middle East and had a Navy as large as that of the U.S.A., a power with whom it had by then been officially declared "war is unthinkable". The phrase really meant that military operations between the U.S.A. and Britain had become unthinkable. We have only to turn our minds back to Suez to observe that a conflict of ideas (war or *werre*) between Washington and London is still quite thinkable.

When World War II broke out the French had inwardly lost the will to defend anything by violence. They were too weak and possibly too civilized to wish to make large-scale war.

The Indo-China struggle, so prolonged and yet so suddenly abandoned, and the Algerian struggle—which seems almost certain to end in some form of Algerian independence—are hangovers from France's attempt to rebuild her Empire after the defeats of the Napoleonic wars. To-day the Nato Commander must often have anxious thoughts about what may happen to his lines of communication through France in the event of a major war.

Of France it can be said that she is lost in a world of naked power politics (as indeed we all are now that power has become nuclear), and would be no less lost and trailing along behind if nuclear weapons did not exist.[1]

Her future can only be bright in a peacefully organized world and then it would be dazzling for, though she is in permanent political and financial disorder, she occupies an

---

[1] Yet in October, 1957 the French were saying that if the disarmament talks at the U.N. failed, France would have to make atomic weapons.

unique and indispensable position and influence in Western civilization. I have often said to my French friends: "What annoys me about you is that in your heart of hearts I know you feel that provided one Frenchman and two women are left alive on earth, Western civilization is safe and I have to admit you are right, even though you collapsed in 1940 and shrugged off a German occupation."

And now the Americans. The American attitude towards defence has been interesting and in many respects unique. It is significant that the strongest power in the world to-day began its history so much later than most other Western powers, and thus built up its traditions during the past 200 years. America was founded to provide men with an escape from what were regarded as the evils of European civilization, particularly the tyranny of Kings and ecclesiastical potentates.

It was the American dream that across the Atlantic Ocean a new kind of society should be created, and it is the inescapable destiny of every American citizen to inherit this noble ideal and unattainable ambition. This has influenced their defence policy.

The British, having passed through the empire-building stage are now (1957) busily divesting themselves of colonies; indeed the granting of self-government to dependent peoples has become one of Britain's principal preoccupations. The Americans have not been inspired by the empire-building urge (the Philippines and dollar diplomacy in S. America were minor falls from grace) though there is no certainty that they might not become interested in it in economic form.

The Monroe Doctrine reflected a desire by the Americans to isolate themselves from the rest of the wicked world. Compelled in 1917 by their urge to be on the side of the angels they intervened (temporarily as they thought) in World War I and then most lamentably retreated again towards the mirage of isolationism when they refused to become members of the League of Nations and disowned the moral leadership of President Wilson. In World War II President Roosevelt worked assiduously and with greater political skill than Wilson to bring the U.S.A. into the battle against the evil ideas, and the Japanese attack on Pearl Harbour clinched the argument between isolationists and interventionists.

After World War II the inescapable reality of the ONE WORLD was accepted by the American people who welcomed the headquarters of the United Nations to New York and committed themselves to its policies. The fabulous aid (military and economic) which the U.S.A. has poured forth to the free world since 1945 has been unprecedented in history. This extraordinary and novel behaviour by a sovereign state has not been sufficiently appreciated by the beneficiaries who have been (and still are) constantly irritated by the short-term tactical political errors of the State Department learning by experience how to deal with the many and perplexing problems consequent upon America's assumption of leadership of the free world. The Americans are also having to learn a lesson well known to the British that "do-gooders" are invariably unpopular.

To sum up: All the American wars have had a strong ideological content. The first a fight for democratic independence; the second a fight for the freedom of the seas; the third a civil war over slavery and the right to secede, and then World Wars I and II, and Korea.

The Americans have always fought in defence of an idea and the idea behind their crusades has been the American dream. Up to and including World War I it seemed natural to Englishmen to expect some tangible gain from winning a war, be it annexation or reparations; that is how it had always been. To the Americans it was equally traditional not to exact reparations because wars were fought to do good or at any rate chiefly to punish and prevent evil. By World War II the British had come round to that way of thinking and all they asked of a Germany which had surrendered unconditionally was that some Nazis should be hanged and that Germans would try very hard to be democrats and eschew militarism.[1]

If we look back over the centuries and consider the objects of the many wars which have splashed the pages of history with blood since the national state idea became commonly accepted as the normal social arrangement, a development is to be observed which can be summarized as follows and is illustrated by the examples outlined in the preceding pages.

[1] It was awkward that Soviet activities obliged the British to ask the Germans to re-arm whilst the Germans were still sitting in sackcloth and ashes contemplating the ruinous consequences of militarism. *"Ohne mich"* was a natural reaction by young Germans.

It is a development which indicates that the differences of opinion or wars (*werre*) between sovereign states have tended to become less about "things" and more about "ideas".

It must be recognized that this is only a tendency, a kind of political drift of the centre of gravity of war-purposes and that it is easy to find plenty of examples in the past where the difference of opinion was largely about ideas, and examples to-day where the difference of opinion between the contestants is chiefly about "things".

Nor would it be right to say that any struggle either in the past or at this time has been exclusively about ideas or things. Furthermore, in a given struggle the balance of emphasis between ideas and things as the chief root of the difference between states may not be the same on each side.

Consider the Algerian war. From the French point of view the emphasis is on "things" such as the properties and homes and businesses of the 1,000,000 French residents and the potentialities of the oil and mineral deposits in the N. Sahara. I doubt whether the French Government or people have any strong feelings about the preservation of the French way of life amongst the Arabs. This is not to deny that there also exists in the France of 1957 a feeling that the retention of control of Algeria is bound up with the question of French prestige as a great power.

From the Arab point of view the prime motive of the rebels is the idea that they would like to govern themselves. The simple idea—but history shows that it is a potent idea—that self-government may be preferable to good government. To this must be added a certain weight of opinion amongst N. African Arabs who, *when* they have achieved political independence, wish to retain French cultural contacts and influences.

Coming now to the attitude of the British it is my belief that we have reached a stage in our historical evolution when we are concerned more with the defence of ideas we cherish than with things. As a boy I was told we "owned" a great Empire on which the sun never set and was shown maps of a world largely coloured red. The idea of "owning" the Empire, inaccurate even in 1900, is now dead except amongst the lunatic fringe and there is a good deal of uncertainty as to what the Commonwealth adds up to. I believe the nation feels that, on the whole, it fought two world wars in defence of the democratic idea and that Russia is the enemy to-day because of its exploitation of the Communist idea, whereas in 1880 Russia was a potential enemy because she was expanding in Central Asia and getting close to the N.W. frontier of "our" Indian Empire, the "brightest jewel in Queen Victoria's Crown".

There is no single and simple explanation for this change in the character of our values. It is a mixture of a great many developments which all fall into two main categories, one a credit to our common sense, the other a credit to our ideals.

In the common-sense category is the fact that we are physically incapable of holding by force, or against the will of other people, possessions or positions which we once regarded as essential to our well-being or our security or our dignity or our pride. From the loss of Calais in 1558 to the enforced evacuation of Suez in 1957 there are plenty of examples of our ability to recognize the facts of life. On the side of morals we have the evolution of the Commonwealth and in particular the grant of independence to the Asian Dominions, and to other colonies such as Ghana and Nigeria. To concede independence to India was inevitable and non-violent resistance in India helped to speed the process, but it was not absolutely or urgently necessary in 1947. If we had been foolish or more wicked than we are it might have been delayed till 1950 or 1955.

I will tell you a short story:

"There was once upon a time a burglar called John Bull who was—according to foreigners—very expert at entering and robbing other people's houses. John Bull was often very puzzled by foreign criticism for, although it was true that he went into other people's property, he often felt that it was in the true interest of the residents as well as of himself that he took this action. He would—once he had taken over the property—open the windows, instal sanitation, teach the owners English and self-government and carry on other beneficial activities from which he could hardly help deriving certain economic advantages, and why not? The 'civilizer' (as he regarded himself) was surely worthy of his hire? As a result of two world wars in which he fought tenaciously and to the point of exhaustion against a very bad type of robber, who had no understanding of what should or should not be done and wished to destroy

John Bull, the latter was informed by his medical adviser that
he had a hernia: 'No more drain-pipe entrances for you, my
boy.' In these circumstances John Bull decided to turn over a
new leaf and become an active supporter of the forces of
international law and allow all the good side of his character
to govern his behaviour. He was by nature quite a good man
and was almost as astonished as anyone else when in a moment
of excitement and the raising of his blood-pressure by Nasser
he forgot his hernia and his morals for a few weeks."

I do not want to push the parable too hard but it illustrates
the change which has come over our policy and the combination of reasons which have motivated our action.

I remind you that the question was: What are we trying to
defend, and against whom and against what are we trying to
defend IT?

My conclusion—for reasons set forth in this chapter—is
that IT is an IDEA comprehended in the phrase OUR WAY OF
LIFE, and that we are trying to defend it against policies of the
Soviet Union which (and here at least there is no room for
doubt) are designed to secure world domination for the Communist way of life. This great ideological struggle for the soul of
man and the allegiance of his heart and mind is a turning-
point in human history. The world in my life-time has shrunk
amazingly in terms of the time space factor; it is—with the
exception of the ocean depths—fully explored, and men's
thoughts are reaching out towards the planets before they have
come to terms with each other about their arrangements on this
globe. But come to terms they must and without much delay,
because at the present rate of "progress" the world has become
ONE for war as well as for peace.[1] World government is now
technically possible even if psychologically we have perhaps
three generations to go. In the functional sphere we are moving
fast because the complex nature of our modern, mechanized
and economically intertwined society, forces us to rationalize
our emotional nationalism and—let it be remembered—the
national-state idea has only been in existence for a few centuries.
It has served its purpose and is on the way out. World Wars I

<hr>

[1] At the Conservative Party Conference in 1957, Mr. Duncan Sandys, Minister
of Defence, said that ultimately "a world authority with a world police force" was
essential.

and II were the beginnings of its end. Whether it will disappear in a final cataclysm is a question whose answer is beyond the horizon of time, but not beyond our power to influence.

To those who doubt we are moving towards world government I recommend the exercise of making a list setting forth the number of international organizations of an official character which existed in 1900 and another list of those operating, some well, some badly, to-day.

We are coming to terms with each other notably in the non-political aspects of our lives; but, as man is a political animal, it is politics which have the last and decisive word.

What are to be the political terms? A democratic or a communist form of world government? That is what the present war is about; that is the great discord and clash of ideas. The World *werre*. We are defending an IDEA expressed by our way of life. This is the IT. To defend it successfully is not only to our self-interest but to the interest of the future of mankind; and *how* we defend it may be an equally important matter. We must now examine the nature of this way of life and describe it, for without this knowledge (and knowledge of the ways it can be attacked) how can we decide which is the best way to defend it?

CHAPTER THREE

OUR WAY OF LIFE

THE CONCLUSION was reached in the last chapter that what we, the people of the United Kingdom, wish to defend is an IDEA which should be described as *our way of life*. Before we consider to what extent our present defence arrangements fulfil this purpose, more must be said about this way of life; its theory and its practice.

Our way of life is rooted in the idea that MAN the individual is the most important element in society. This conception is expressed in the phrase that "the state exists for Man and not Man for the state".

"I think; therefore I am," said Descartes. The significance of the human personality is bound up with the conception of freedom, since without freedom this personality cannot express itself.

The question to be considered is whether Man is naturally freedom loving? An affirmative answer must to some extent be based on faith, but history is often the story of the ceaseless struggle of groups of men to liberate themselves from what they conceived to be unreasonable control by others.

In recent times the world has witnessed the operation of the Fascist, Nazi and Communist dictatorships. It was believed by some people that, if a generation of a nation had never known freedom, had never been taught what democracy was, nor what the individual's duty was in a democracy but had, on the contrary, been taught that the Communist creed and practices were the true expression of democracy, then it was impossible to expect a generation thus conditioned would want true freedom or make any move to obtain it.

For how, it was argued, could a man want something he knew nothing about, or feel the absence of privileges he had never known? But 1956 saw the Hungarian rising against the Communist tyranny, a revolt of which the students, the writers and other intellectuals were the mainspring of what became a national rising and, even after it was suppressed by Russian brutality, a psychological resistance continued to be maintained by the youth.

"Liberty"—wrote Professor Massimo Salvadori, in *Liberal Democracy*—"is free choice, each individual's own decision concerning his course of action; it belongs to man himself, not to the external world which surrounds him."

But since MAN does not live alone, account must be taken of the personalities of other men and, unless we accept the doctrine of Anarchy, the individual must give weight to the desires and personalities of others, recognize that they are no less important from the point of view of the maintenance of freedom than his own and also realize that he must develop his own personality and ability in harmony with the development of other men.

This social need leads to what at first sight appears to be restrictions on liberty, but restrictions in some directions are necessary in order that there shall be freedom in others.

A simple but practical example is provided by the need for traffic control. Restrictive rules, regulations and penalties for infractions are essential if men are to be free to move from place to place in an orderly and speedy manner. The problem of determining the correct balance between control and freedom is the continuous problem confronting those peoples who believe as we do that a kind of society we call democratic is the best way of ensuring the maximum possible and practical degree of personal freedom.

The essence of a democratic way of life is that the people as a whole should determine the extent and degree to which, in the interests of the liberty of the individual, the State, representing the whole community, should control the freedom of that individual. In order to achieve this purpose democratic institutions have been created and they should be judged by the extent to which they maximize the liberty of the individual to develop his personality in harmony with those of others. Democracy must not be thought of as something which can be achieved once and for all. It is a system or way of life in which the individual has responsibilities as well as rights and in which growth is needed if achievements are to be preserved and enlarged. Democracy demands the loyalty and services of the individual who must of his own free will and from inner conviction accept the personal responsibility of making democracy "work"; of preserving its principles; of defending it against internal and external enemies. Unless buttressed by acceptance of personal responsibilities which put content into rights, the latter will disappear.

Above all it must be remembered that democracy is not created or given life by constitutions or the machinery of government.

Democracy must and can only thrive if its roots go down into the hearts and minds of individuals. Unless democratic institutions are themselves inspired by democratic principles they can become not the servants but the masters and even the destroyers of democracy. This may be because such institutions tend to develop a corporate personality, and indeed require to do so in order to be efficient, and the body corporate has an instinctive hostility towards the body personal.

To the Government Department "the public" is to be esteemed because collectively it has a consumer value from the angle of the department's activities, but the individual can be a nuisance.

Furthermore the body corporate will always take the "larger view" which on technical grounds enables it to make out a good case for ignoring the just claims of individual or minority interests. However specious the technical argument may be that some individual point of view be brushed aside it will often be found that the apparent gains in efficiency have been made at the cost of whittling away the reality of an important democratic principle.

Where the balance lies in particular cases must be a matter of personal judgment but, when in doubt—and doubts should be always alert—it is wisest to give liberty the benefit of the doubt.

II

It has been said that a democratic society is like an elephant; it is hard to define but easy to recognize when one sees it. Some of the outward and visible signs which demonstrate that we are living in a democracy in the United Kingdom are described below.

First there is the institution of Parliament. It is not always

understood, even by M.P.'s, that the purpose of Parliament is
not to make laws but to prevent the executive (which is or
should be the creature of Parliament) from being given more
power (through legislation) than it requires to do its job of
governing the nation. *As much power as is essential; but no more*,
and in theory every backbench M.P. should adopt a critical
attitude to the demand of the Executive for more power.

This is not the place to discourse about the function of
Parliament, but this institution is undoubtedly the central,
most conspicuous and—one might add—world famous of all
the outward and visible signs of the ideas which inspire our
way of life in the United Kingdom. But, when later on we shall
come to a consideration of the methods of defence of our way of
life and whether it can be done by more than one method, we
must not forget that even Parliament is only the crowning
summit of a series of discussions about government of which
not the least important may be heard going on most evenings
in the village pubs.

A free Press is another generally accepted characteristic of a
democratic society, though again it would exceed the limits of
this book to attempt to describe its functions in a free society.
Freedom to believe in and practise any religion or none; freedom of association and speech; all these are amongst the
generally accepted features of a democratic society.

But it can hardly be over-emphasized that these freedoms
will not exist, and if once established can easily wither away
and die and be replaced by tyranny, unless the majority of the
individuals in a society believe in these freedoms and are prepared to be vigilant and take appropriate action if the freedoms
are in jeopardy from enemies within and without.

I remarked earlier that a democratic way of life can easily
be recognized when it is seen or experienced and the same
applies to a totalitarian régime.

In Britain, for example, it is only necessary for a visitor to
spend an hour during question time in the House of Commons
to have ample proof that the British Parliament is a free
institution. A few hours listening to radio programmes in the
U.S.A. provides a striking contrast to a study of Russian radio.

No claim is being made that the free way of life as we know
it in the U.K. and other democratic countries has achieved

perfection; very far from it. For instance racialism in the U.S.A., telephone tapping in Britain or (a Cypriot might say) British policy in Cyprus, French policy in Algeria are all matters providing ammunition for critics; but the fact that all these activities are the subject of public debate in the countries concerned is proof of the democratic nature of the social climate.

Recently I asked a senior Russian official why the B.B.C. broadcasts to Russia were jammed. After some evasions he said with a smile: "Britain jammed the Athens radio in Cyprus." My comment, to which he had no reply, was: "I agree, but I was able to write an article in England criticizing this policy; could anyone write an article in *Pravda* criticizing your policy?"

Obviously all human endeavour must fall short of perfection but of the free way of life, of which the expression of the wills of the people through some form of freely elected parliamentary institution is an imperfect feature, it can be said in words Sir Winston Churchill once used: "It may have its defects but no one has yet been able to invent a better one." I am not, however, concerned in this book with an examination of the merits or short-comings of the free way of life. My purpose must be limited to setting down a sufficient account of what it is to enable the reader to assess it in terms of understanding what has to be defended; what in short is the nature of the object of our defence expenditures? In terms of a military appreciation our way of life as an object to be defended falls into two inter-related parts.

First there is the IDEA and this idea, this conception of the significance of the individual, is the foundation of the whole business and its face, house, citadel, fortress or centre is the mind and personality of the individual. *If this is lost to the enemy all is lost. If this citadel can be denied to the enemy hope must not be abandoned: victory is still possible.*

It will be remembered that when in Chapter I we discussed the nature of war it was argued that in the last analysis war (werre) was a conflict of ideas and that total victory as contrasted with military victory was not achieved until, through one means or another, the enemy had changed his mind and genuinely accepted the views to which he had been hostile. In an ideological struggle between (say) democratic and Communist ideas the ultimate and decisive battlefield is to be found

in the minds of the contestants and the action of the governments must be supposed to reflect the collective opinion of the
nation. It is of the essence of democracy that this must be so in
a democratic state and the extent to which this is true in a
totalitarian state must depend upon the degree to which the
people have been misled and/or terrorized into supporting the
actions of totalitarian government.

Therefore I assert that in considering the defence of the
British way of life *it is the freedom idea which is the ark of the
covenant* and for this to survive at least one man or woman
must continue to cherish it and hold on to it *at all cost*. But to
be practical one must say that for the freedom idea to survive
in terms of real politics there must exist a substantial part of the
nation, and preferably a majority thereof, composed of individuals who believe in the idea and are prepared to support
a government which will do something about defending it.

Secondly, our way of life is also composed of the institutions
such as Parliament, the Press, the law courts applying democratically made laws, the B.B.C. and television, the Churches,
and the multitude of free institutions and societies which include
world famous bodies and the smallest village club or regular
gathering of friends in the local.

This way of life we desire to defend can be summed up in
these words: it has a spiritual basis which can be thought of as
millions of roots each nurtured and deriving life from an
individual's consciousness. These roots rise up to support a great
tree of which the central trunk is Parliament and the branches,
twigs and leaves are the institutions of our free society. Two
pamphlets which contain much wisdom on the great subject
touched upon in this chapter are *Education for Liberty*,[1] and *The
Meaning of Freedom*.[2]

When all is said and done the most practical way by which
the average citizen can appreciate what we mean by our way
of life and what it means to us, is by studying conditions in
totalitarian states, by reading objective reports about those
conditions, talking to people who have escaped from tyranny
and projecting himself into the atmosphere of such social
conditions; then contrasting it with conditions in a truly
democratic country.

[1] By Massimo Salvadori, 3s. 6d.   [2] (A symposium) 3s. 6d.   Pall Mall Press.

CHAPTER FOUR

THE ATTACK ON OUR WAY OF LIFE

A SOUND PLAN OF defence must be related to the anticipated nature of the attack. In the wide definition of war (werre) to which we must accustom ourselves, i.e. a clash of ideas between sovereign states, the attack does not begin when and if the ideological struggle degenerates into military operations. It starts earlier. Therefore in considering the nature of the attack against which we must defend our way of life we can distinguish two problems; one political and the other military. (Battle of Brains and Battle of Bodies.) The emphasis which the enemy will place on each of these two methods will vary from struggle to struggle.

Few will deny that Hitler and the Nazi movement were a menace to our way of life. But the Nazi attack was more associated with violence than with political operations. It is true that there were Nazi-type organizations outside Germany, such as Mosley's Black Shirts in Britain, the Croix de Feu group in France and the Fascist régime in Italy, but according to Mussolini "Fascism was not for export"; he had other ideas about Italian Imperialism. The Nazis never made much effort to build up satellite Nazi parties in foreign countries. The "fifth columns" were treacherous organizations rather than political parties. The Nazi menace to our way of life was principally expressed in the form of territorial expansion and hence the strengthening of the military resources of the German Reich which carried with it (wherever it obtained control) totalitarian ideas and practices and anti-semitism. This policy of expansion was promoted by force or the threat of force.

The Communist menace has followed a different policy. Political activity in order to obtain adherents to an international organization controlled and directed by the Communist Party of the Soviet Union has been the spearhead of the offensive against democracy. Force has been used as a supporting and consolidating influence. This is the policy laid down by Soviet Communist leaders as the theoretically correct strategy and it has usually been followed in practice.[1] It has been remarkably successful, partly because the potential victims (the democratic states) were not prepared for or organized to deal with this kind of war. They have been as ill-equipped to cope with what they have come to call the cold war as they were to deal militarily with the Nazi blitzkrieg into Western Europe in 1940.

This policy of "peaceful" persuasion and infiltration is well adapted to operations in uncommitted states who, at an early stage in their development, cannot be classified as being in either the democratic or Communist camp. Communism has some attractive features to the rulers of these countries because it supplies the excuse for authoritarian government which has technical advantages in an undeveloped country and at the same time claims to be ultra-democratic—a label which has great prestige value. I cannot think of any government which boasts that it is *not* democratic.

Our defence policy to deal with the attack on our way of life must therefore be capable of dealing with two types of tactics, the political and the military, of which the political is Moscow's favourite child.

II

The political attack (in which I include the economic) by Russian leaders on our way of life in particular and the free way of life in general is conducted by two methods, both directed towards the same objective. The first method includes all the measures appropriate to building up in the society of the prospective victim a strong Communist Party; the second part of the business is of a more general character designed to produce an international opinion favourable to the Soviet Union and the Communist doctrine.

The local Communist Party takes its orders from Moscow and operates above and below ground. It will fight elections and endeavour to capture the Parliamentary system; it will seek to penetrate all forms of organizations especially the Trade

---

[1] See *The Communist Conspiracy* by S. King-Hall (Constable). A book based on the statements of Communists.

Unions, the Civil Services and associations of intellectuals and youth movements. It will also operate at various levels underground from the depths of espionage to the fomentation of industrial unrest and various degrees of sabotage.

The second method of political attack includes the creation of world wide organizations ostensibly ultra-democratic but actually agencies of the Soviet Government.[1] Also in this department of the political attack are the anti-imperialist political and economic activities amongst the Middle Eastern, Asian and African peoples, activities which aim at exploiting the emotion of nationalism, so that a belief in nationalism and a belief in Communism seem to be the same thing.

The military attack on the free way of life has not as a rule taken the form of armed intervention. The Soviet Union has maintained extremely powerful military forces and has not hesitated to use them in cases when, as in East Germany and Hungary, servile Communist governments called for outside assistance against a population in revolt. But it seems that the controllers of Soviet policy are aware of the difficulties which arise in attempts to impose ideas by force and that, unless one is careful, such operations may defeat their own ends by rallying the people against the foreign invader.[2]

Since World War II Russian conventional forces have been and still are far superior to anything which could be mustered by the West, and therefore since 1946 a Russian conventional invasion of Western Europe would have been a fairly easy operation. Whether or not any ideas they had about this method of extending the Western frontier of Communism during the period 1945-51 were set aside because of the—at that time—Western monopoly of the atomic bomb must be a matter of opinion.

My own guess is that they preferred to rely on the hope that Communist parties would by more or less legitimate means gain control of France and Italy, a development which might well have occurred but for Marshall Aid.

I believe the proceedings of the 20th Congress of the Communist Party indicated that it had become recognized in

---

[1] They are numerous. The World Federation of Trade Unions and the World Peace Council are typical examples.

[2] See page 46.

C

Moscow that Stalin had made a serious tactical error by allowing a military situation to develop which so alarmed the West that they were scared into creating Nato.

At the moment of writing I detect no change in the general strategy of the Communist attack and no obvious reason why it should change from being primarily a political or subversive form of attack into direct military attack.

The White Paper on Defence 1957 says in para 15 that "the free world is to-day mainly dependent for its *protection* upon the nuclear capacity of the United States" (italics mine). The authors of the White Paper could claim that the word "protection" is only meant to refer to physical attack, and that they are not so foolish as to suggest that the nuclear capacity of the U.S.A. protects the free world from political attack.

My comment on this would be that according to para 3 "the Communist threat remains, but its nature has changed". Changed from what into what? We are not told. There is however a reference in para 27 to "Communist encroachment and infiltration" in the Baghdad Pact area, followed by the observation that British forces *"including Bomber Squadrons based in Cyprus capable of delivering nuclear weapons"* would be made available to support the Alliance. It is not clear to me how the Cyprus based bombers prevent Communist infiltration in the Baghdad Pact area.

In writing a book of this kind its author is necessarily several months behind events but, whilst this chapter was in first draft, two events occurred which illustrated in a striking manner the Communist technique of using military potential to support political and economic penetration.

The first was the news that the Soviet Union had "penetrated" Syria, providing arms, technicians and economic aid. Before this could take place effective power in Syria had to be in the hands of Communists or near Communists, or non-Communists who did not see the dangers of an embrace by the Russian Bear. As part of the whole operation a plot was "discovered" purporting to be an American plan to dominate Syria. The news that the Russians had leap-frogged the Baghdad Pact seems (as usual) to have taken the Western powers by surprise, and it became painfully obvious that there was nothing they could do about the Russian coup. The two instruments of defence in their hands were useless. One was the American 6th Fleet with nuclear weapons; the other was the R.A.F. at Cyprus with planes that could carry nuclear weapons. It was apparent to the world in general, and the Middle East states in particular, that the Eisenhower doctrine and the statement in the Defence Paper which I have italicized were devoid of substance.

The conclusion is inescapable that in this typical case the defence arrangements of the West were unrelated to the nature of the Russian attack.

The second illustration was the timing in connection with the disarmament talks in London of the Russian announcement that they had tested an inter-continental guided missile. It was a masterly stroke of political warfare.[1]

In endeavouring to estimate the correct answer to this question about the type of attack or attacks on our way of life, against which we must have appropriate defences, the first consideration is that the life-force of our way of life is the IDEA (freedom, etc.); we must therefore suppose that from the Soviet point of view their offensive will be concentrated against the decisive point which is the IDEA. It is axiomatic that the most potent weapon with which to attack an idea is another idea and this supports the expectation that it is in the sphere of political warfare that we should expect to find the weight of the Soviet attack, and that our defences must take account of this fact. When I write *defences* it is assumed that attack on our part is recognized as being an essential part of our defence.

It is within this context that Soviet military force is an important factor in the general strategy of their attack, in which it is—on the whole—used indirectly. We must therefore examine what place our military force should occupy in the over-all picture of our defence arrangements.

[1] An even smarter coup was the sudden launching of the first Russian satellite. This was a great tactical victory in the Battle of the Brains. The despatch of an even larger satellite containing the dog also made a great impression. We are now living under a new and sinister sign of the Zodiac, number 13: "The sign of the Dead Dog" (1957).

CHAPTER FIVE

THE ROLE OF MILITARY FORCE

I HAVE ARGUED that at this time in our history the prime purpose of the defence policy of the United Kingdom (in association with like-minded peoples) is to defend a way of life.[1] This conception of defending a system of government, a free way of life, has recently emerged historically as an addition to the traditional notion that the chief purpose of defence was to safeguard things material, in particular the integrity of the homeland. Our way of life is a combination of institutions and ideas and, although the existence of the institutions (Parliament, free Press, etc.) is almost indispensable to the practice and application of our way of life, it is the IDEA itself which is the heart of the matter. Because this idea has its shrine in the heart and mind of the individual, the IDEA of the free way of life is indestructible so long as there are individuals who are determined not to surrender morally and therefore refuse to abandon their beliefs.

It is the purpose of this chapter to enquire what contribution military force can make to this conception of the defence of a way of life. The last chapter outlined the methods by which we may expect our way of life to be attacked and it was shown that they fell into two inter-related categories, the political and the military. What role can military force play in our defence policy against each of these types of assault? First consider political attack.

The use of armed force by anti-democratic powers in the sphere of political warfare is usually of a supporting and exploiting character. At some stage, when political warfare operations have created a political climate in the democratic country so that a non-democratic group has seized power, either through apathy of the democratic section of the nation or by resolute action culminating in a *coup d'état*, armed force

---

[1] The objective of defending our way of life is specifically mentioned in the Defence Statement of 1955 and by implication in the 1956 Statement.

from outside can be used as a means of supporting the total-itarian régime or, as in the case of the riots in East Germany and the Hungarian rising, be used to rescue an already estab-lished régime if it is in danger of losing control.

Nevertheless the use of armed force by a Communist state in an ideological struggle with democratic elements has dis-advantages from the point of view of the Communists since it is a public confession of failure to win the battle of ideas. One must await the verdict of history in order to determine exactly whether the Russian decision to go with armed force to the support of their Communist agents in Hungary was a wise move. It is true that within a few weeks the rising was crushed and a subservient Communist government re-established in full tyranny but, on the other side of the balance sheet the utmost confusion was created in the ranks of the Communist parties in the democratic countries, world public opinion was outraged and the duplicity of Russian peaceful propaganda was exposed.

Furthermore the Hungarian rising (and the more artfully operated Polish liberation movement) must have made the Russian general staff acutely aware of the difficulties they would have on their lines of communication through the states of Eastern Europe in the event of a Russian invasion into Western Europe.

The blow to the non-Russian Communist parties (already shaken by the denunciation of Stalinism) was very severe when sincere Communists discovered that Russian armed forces had shot down workers in Hungary, and all over the world there were desertions from the C.P. of persons who could not accept the view that the Hungarian rising was a Fascist plot. In exposing the truth the U.N. report played an important role and the frantic efforts of the Communist régime in Hungary to counteract it by all kinds of devices was evidence of their realization that it was a very damaging document.

We are inclined in the West to pay too much attention to our domestic difficulties and overlook those of the enemy, which is perhaps evidence of the success of their political warfare strategy. If we imagine what it would mean to our cause if, in every Communist state, we knew there were an organized and legally recognized democratic party of dedicated men and women taking their line from (say) the Council of Nato, one would begin to appreciate the importance to Moscow of foreign Communist parties (especially in France and Italy) and that the confusion into which these parties were thrown by the Hungarian affair, a confusion from which they will find it hard to recover, is something for which Hungarians have not died in vain.

Before we leave the question of the utility of armed force as a defence mechanism in the political warfare battle it is right to point out that the conclusion reached that military force is not of great significance in this aspect of the defence of our way of life applies particularly to Britain and to other nations where the Communist party is of small significance.

Although one must be careful not to be too sure that anything "cannot happen here", it seems unlikely that in the United Kingdom conditions in any foreseeable future will favour the rise to power of a British Communist party relying at some critical moment upon the support of Russian armed force. It is not a danger for which we need large armed forces. In France and Italy, where there are large and well organized Communist parties, the supporters of democracy feel that they have to take into account the possibility of a *coup d'état* and that democracy must have considerable armed force with which to deal with a revolution.

This may be true but calls for two comments. First the more certain way of defending the democratic way of life in such countries is to find out what are the reasons which cause tens of thousands of citizens to support Communism and remove those reasons; secondly, that the strength and character of armed forces required to maintain law and order and protect the democratic nature of the state against internal revolutionary elements is quite different from those armed forces intended to operate internationally.

Tactical atomic weapons have not *yet* become conventional weapons for the suppression of riots!

The second line of attack on our way of life, viz. physical assault by the enemy armed forces, is an assault which can be anything from hostile economic pressure to all-out nuclear war.

Although it has been agreed that this type of assault on our way of life is not regarded by Communists as the most desirable tactic, we cannot exclude its possibility. Internal political problems might make Soviet leaders feel that an armed assault on the West, described as a preventive war to forestall the aggressive intention of the Imperialist powers, would be a necessary move to distract the attention of their people from internal troubles. Furthermore there may be something (I should guess not much) in the argument that if large forces exist, Generals, Admirals and Air Marshals have a feeling they would like to try them out. In my experience senior serving officers are sometimes more pacifically-minded than politicians.

There is also the ever-present danger—and, as we shall see later on the existence of nuclear weapons adds weight to this particular danger—that the Soviet leaders may be emboldened to pursue or encourage an aggressive political or economic policy because they believe they can go a very long way before passing the point of no return which causes the dispute to become military in character. A very aggressive Soviet political policy in the Middle East might so stir up nationalist passions that a local war involving Turkey and Syria or Israel and Arab states might become military with unpredictable consequences.

There can be no disputing the fact that if nation A has a way of life which nation B is endeavouring to destroy and nation A has no armed force, or a force manifestly inferior to that of nation B, the latter can impose its will on nation A in all material matters. Nation B can occupy the territory of nation A and then endeavour to impose upon its nationals the way of life believed in by B and abhorred by A.

The occupation of a democratic country by the forces of a totalitarian state is a serious matter for the occupied nation. There is a sense of humiliation and defeat and morale is lowered; the institutions of the free way of life are suppressed; Parliament is abolished or replaced by a façade; the freedom of the Press and radio disappears; free speech becomes dangerous; individuals, perhaps many thousands of individuals, are deported, imprisoned, tortured and perhaps executed. In short, the enemy is in a powerful position from which to destroy the organization of its opponents' way of life and, unless long and careful efforts have been made to prepare the nation to grapple with this novel situation, many individuals, perhaps the majority, will despair, will lose faith in their way of life and even come to the conclusion that the enemy's way is, after all, the best, or one to which there is no practical alternative.

All the hardships mentioned above have usually followed upon the military defeat of the forces of the occupied territory; but not always. Iceland was occupied by the British and Americans in World War II, although the island had declared for permanent neutrality in 1918, and Denmark was occupied by the Germans after negligible military action. But these were exceptional cases. When an enemy occupation takes place as a result of military defeat it requires great resolution on the part of the people and its leaders not to suppose that all is lost. Indeed, since it has hitherto usually been considered that the integrity of the homeland was the be-all and end-all of defence, it is not surprising that an occupation has usually been regarded as the end of the war and, at the best, most of the occupied people have only thought in terms of being liberated. They hoped that some other power, using armed forces, would drive out the occupier.

A military force capable of denying to the enemy the ability, either through an occupation or blockade, to impose his terms on the democratic nation is a very useful asset in the business of defending one's way of life and an essential requirement for the maintenance of the normal institutions of the free way of life. It is possible to live in a state of near nakedness in almost any climate if trained and prepared for the job, but adequate clothing and shelter make living much easier, and if a person accustomed to these amenities is suddenly stripped naked in a harsh climate and has *not* been trained to meet this contingency, then he will probably die. So it is with the practice of our democratic way of life. Its material coverings can be helpful to its security, but it should not be assumed that it cannot continue to live without the institutions, if it is sufficiently well established in the hearts and minds of individuals. Indeed unless the free way of life *is* solidly established in the minds of individuals the existence of material prosperity does not guarantee the security of the free way of life; it can jeopardize it.

Although a good case can be made for the use of force to protect the institutions and public practice of our way of life, its use inevitably carries with it certain disadvantages. First there are the political and psychological consequences of using force *on a large scale*. Such force on the scale used in a world war (as contrasted with police operations) demands that the nation be organized in a total manner. The executive rightly insists that it must be given powers of control in the national emergency far exceeding anything normally considered reasonable according to our way of life. Individuals are imprisoned without trial; the operation of Habeas Corpus is suspended; all property is at the disposal of the state; the Press is censored; the lives and labour of the citizen are subject to the direction of the state. In defence of this abandonment of the principles and practices of our way of life it was argued for example in Britain in World War II, that it was necessary temporarily to put freedoms into cold storage in order to preserve them for posterity, and that the abandonment of freedoms and the granting of dictatorial powers to the executive was a voluntary act undertaken by Parliament, the sovereign body. This was quite true and nothing illustrates more clearly the deep-seated attachment of the British to their way of life than the immense efforts which were made, and on the whole successfully, to give the executive all the power it required whilst at the same time not abandoning the final authority of Parliament.[1]

No more impressive example exists in British history of the reality of our free way of life and what we mean by it in practice than the historic occasion in 1940 when a Parliament (of which the writer had the honour and privilege to be a member), changed the executive. On the other side of the balance sheet some of us thought that we were getting rather near the point of no return when an M.P. could be (and was) incarcerated without trial on the *fiat* of the Home Secretary. Nor was the stupid treatment of aliens in a panicky period in 1940 creditable, but, as mentioned on page 47, in general the British people's attitude to the enemy people was very sane in World War II.

By and large "our way of life" was maintained to an extraordinary degree from 1939-45 and, as the Prime Minister was the first to proclaim, this was a source of great inner national strength. In the U.S.A. the record in World War II was not so good; one has an impression—confirmed by the career of the late Senator McCarthy—that when our transatlantic friends

[1] See *Emergency Powers and the Parliamentary Watchdog: Parliament and the Executive 1939-51* by John Eaves, Jr. (Hansard Society for Parliamentary Government).

get alarmed about any threats to the American way of life they are not over-particular as to how far they deviate from the principles of that way of life (the American Constitution and all that) when they apply defensive measures. Their treatment of American-born Japanese was discreditable.

The use of armed force to defend a way of life against armed attack from without (or within) inevitably carries with it a danger that the remedy may become as obnoxious as the disease; in Britain this danger has hitherto been recognized and kept under control.

A second disadvantage is inherent in the use of armed force as a means of defence against a military attack on the institutions of our way of life. We have seen that its use has certain political risks and we must now enquire into its material disadvantages. The political and material disadvantages are interdependent to the extent to which the effort needed to produce the necessary force is significant in the political and economic life of the nation.

In days when the amount of armed force required for the defence of Britain was provided by small professional armies and navies, a war, even of the magnitude of the struggle against Napoleon, did not involve a tremendous upheaval in the normal life of the nation. But World Wars I and II were of a different order and produced serious effects on the U.K. economy. Apart from the loss of life which was very heavy in World War I, much of the capital accumulated during the nineteenth century was expended and by 1945 the British had paid a heavy material price in defence of liberty. France, already exhausted by her efforts in World War I, was revealed in 1940 as being incapable of supporting the burden of another, but Britain was still able to face up to one more world war. By 1956-57 the facts about Britain's military strength, which had long been obvious to thoughtful people but ignored or evaded by the bulk of the nation, were publicly exposed both by Suez and by the government decision to make substantial cuts in our defence expenditure.

The White Paper on Defence 1957 says with candour: "Britain's influence in the world depends first and foremost on the health of her internal economy and the success of her export trade . . . it is therefore in the true interests of defence that the claims of military expenditure should be considered in conjunction with the need to maintain the country's financial and economic strength" (para 6).

The phrase "in conjunction with" should have been "in subordination to the need to maintain the country's financial and economic strength" upon which, according to the opening sentences of the paragraph, British influence (and by implication, the maintenance of our way of life) depends *first and foremost*. Therefore the use of military force to defend our way of life is of dubious value if, in order to produce effective force against a possible military attack on the institutions of our life (i.e. an invasion of our homeland or a blockade), we have over-strained our economy to breaking point.

We must guard against the danger of going bankrupt because we have taken out a policy against death duties which demands a premium exceeding our income. Although there are good reasons for supposing that the Soviet leaders are finding the economic strain of the present armaments race a considerable handicap in their efforts to raise the standards of living of the people, we should not ignore the possibility that they calculate that to put the screws of military defence expenditure on their peoples is easier for them than it is for the governments in democratic nations. They may therefore feel that an endurance test in armaments expenditure may properly be considered a tactic in the cold war which would produce dividends in the shape of political tensions in the democratic countries, especially those in which there are strong Communist parties who are by definition "peace-loving" and "fighters for peace".

The two disadvantages so far mentioned which are inherent in the use of force as a means of defence are not novel but have been becoming more significant as the scale and tempo of violence between states at war has increased and the area of the battlefield has extended towards world-wide dimensions.

If the amount and equality of force which has to be used to counter the force of the enemy exceeds a certain magnitude, we approach a state of affairs in which the destruction produced by the clash of forces is so immense that once again our cure may be worse than the disease. If, for example, in order to prevent any enemy occupation of the homeland and consequent destruction of the institutions of our way of life, we must accept a clash of force of a magnitude likely to destroy the institutions *and* a large number of individuals as well, perhaps 30 per cent of the nation, or even 60 per cent, then there does not seem to be much purpose in the operation. It may be true we should not be occupied, but then neither should we exist in order to benefit from not being occupied.

*   *   *

To complete this examination of the role of force in the defence of our free way of life we must consider the offensive use of force which, in the hands of our enemies, is employed as a kind of reserve to their political warfare operations. For example, many observers detected in September 1957 a relationship between the upsurge of toughness in the Soviet's diplomacy and their claim to have fired an intercontinental rocket.

How can force be of use to the democracies in their counter-offensive; in their attack on the enemy?

We cannot use force for the purposes of a preventive war without compromising our democratic principles, and this greatly handicaps our freedom of action.

Before the nuclear age force could be used to counter violent aggression without necessarily running a grave risk, or incurring the certainty that the remedy would be worse than the disease; but we had to wait till the enemy used it first.

We could have rescued Abyssinia from Mussolini and Czechoslovakia from Hitler if our forces had been so superior to the aggressor that he would have suffered an immediate military defeat and *if we had had the will to use force*. Quite apart from the size of our forces, the will to go further than economic sanctions (less oil) against Mussolini, and even to go as far as that against Hitler, was lacking. Why? Because between the world wars the shadow of the bomber was causing men to reflect upon the growing violence of military operations and the certainty that in "the next world war" they would extend into civilian life.

The nuclear age has immensely increased these apprehensions. If the Hungarian revolt had occurred in 1950 when the democracies had a monopoly of atomic weapons, would we have threatened (and meant it) the Soviet Union with atomic attack if they did not keep out of Hungary? I doubt it.

In considering what role armed force can play in our political warfare operations against the enemy people, there is this to be said: Democratic political warfare can only depend on the free conversion of men's minds for its victories, the use of force by the democracies must be limited to ensuring—in appropriate circumstances—that free discussion can take place. When the German nation surrendered unconditionally to superior force it was absurd to suppose that we could *impose* a democratic form of government, and still less a democratic mode of thought, on the German people. We could and did hang the principal personalities associated with the ideas and practices we regarded as evil, but whether this was a wise use of force in support of a campaign to convert the Germans to the free way of life, is a matter of opinion. It seems to me that the Nuremburg trials were a mistake because they were based on the non-democratic procedure of retrospective legislation. It is easier to be fairly confident that the Treaty of Versailles was a mistaken use of the dominant position provided by superior force.

As mentioned above, a preventive war (military phase) by a democratic state is politically indefensible and the democracies have to suffer the disadvantage (in the realm of force) of waiting to be attacked. If they are able to muster sufficient force to beat back and defeat the totalitarians and thus find themselves in possession of the political initiative, their policy should be closely related to democratic principles. They should say in effect: "We have used force but it was against our will because we believe it is an undemocratic manner of settling disputes; we only did so in self-defence against the aggression of your government. We have destroyed your force and now we shall show you by our conduct towards you what democracy means and how different it is from what your totalitarian government would have done to us if its force had prevailed." In brief, the force of the victorious democracies should only be used to ensure that the people of the defeated totalitarian nation are free to develop democracy.

How else can our armed force be useful? Can it help in the struggle for the allegiance of the uncommitted nations? The use of armed force to counter Soviet political attack in these countries seems to have very limited possibilities and involves very grave risks since, if our enemy is conducting a political and/or economic offensive in such a country, the use of armed

force from outside is likely to enable the Communists to raise
the cry of foreign aggression and capitalize the forces of
nationalism. In this connection I had a talk with a Minister of
Defence in a European democratic country in which there was
at that time a real apprehension that the numerous Communist
Party which was known to have stores of arms might attempt
to seize power. In that country were considerable American
forces and the Minister said that in the event of trouble it was
essential that the Americans should not "come to our rescue, or
nine out of ten of our people will become Communists overnight."

The conclusions I have reached after examining the problem
of what contribution armed force can make to the defence of
our way of life in relation to: (*a*) the political attack against
the IDEA, (*b*) the military attack against the institution and
integrity of the homeland, and (*c*) our political offensive against
Communism are these:

First, that so far as Great Britain is concerned, large-scale
military force capable of taking part in global war serves no
useful purpose as a defence against Soviet *political attack*. That
in states where the free way of life is less well established an
adequate armed force of police character may be needed to
prevent an attempt by domestic totalitarians to seize power by
violence.

Secondly, that subject to conditions being fulfilled which are
listed below, armed force can protect the institutions of our
way of life against military attack.

The conditions are these:

(1) The force required to do the job must not be so costly
that its maintenance brings economic ruin to the nation, an
event which would probably lead to the collapse of the institutions of the free way of life.

(2) We must take care that we do not have to so transform
our institutions in order to use the force needed to protect
them that they lose their fundamental purpose of expressing
the idea of our way of life.

(3) The force required must not be so enormously destructive
that (assuming, as we must, that the enemy is using force of
comparable size) the net result is chaos in which the institutions
disappear and a chaos so grave that the elemental urges of

individual survival overcome any desire or hope of preserving the idea of our way of life. There is a fundamental difference between a situation in which for example Parliament cannot function because London is in ruins and one in which Parliament does not function because its members have been arrested.

Thirdly, that whereas the Communist can use force as a backing for the spearhead of his political attack if this attack runs into trouble, because the Communist (even if he prefers to do it psychologically) is in fact imposing his way of life on his victims, the democracies cannot "impose" democracy on anyone and remain true to their principles. They can do no more with force (and this was revealed in the pre-nuclear age) in a country they have subjugated than use such force as may be needed to ensure a state of affairs in which democratic ideas can take root and grow up. The victorious democratic power can, as it were, act—probably only for a short time—as an alien policeman. It can within rather narrow limits punish the guilty, but it is better if this is carried out by the nation which has suffered military defeat. It cannot, under modern conditions, exact reparations, but on the contrary is more likely both on grounds of humanity and self-interest to come to the economic rescue of its defeated enemy.

Those who find some of these arguments difficult to accept, should consider the following facts. In 1946-47 Western Germany was in a state of catastrophic chaos and mental despair unequalled in the history of modern times. She had surrendered unconditionally and lay prostrate amidst the ruins of her cities. Ten years later the £ sterling was fighting for its life; the D Mark sat at the High Table with the $ and the Swiss franc. Without the promised contribution of armed force from W. Germany, Nato was unable to attain even the modest degree of military strength accepted as the minimum (with tactical nuclear weapons) in 1958.

As a friend of mine put it, with a puzzled look on his face: "Dammit, am I dreaming, or did we beat them in 1945? It simply does not add up!"

Now comes the great question. How do our military forces to-day measure up to the roles which it is within the power of armed force to play in the cause of defending our way of life?

CHAPTER SIX

OUR MILITARY DEFENCE

FEW PEOPLE, IF asked: "For what chief purpose does the U.K. spend £1,500 million annually on defence?" would reply: "To defend our way of life." Many would reply: "To defend this country and its overseas possessions."

There is an underlying assumption in all defence talk and thought that the integrity of the homeland is an essential feature of her defence. In the case of Britain, owing to her dependence upon sea communications, the control and defence of the sea routes are essential to the defence of our island home.

If the fundamental purpose of defence is something material, a necessary act of defence is the operation of denying the enemy access to the island kingdom, or preventing him from blockading its ports.

Blücher, on visiting London for the first time, is supposed to have said: "What a city to sack!"

If we are to regard the looting of Britain or the carrying off into slavery and forced labour of a large number of its inhabitants as the only contingencics against which we must defend ourselves, an enemy occupation of Britain will mean that our defences have failed. But material considerations are not the only, or even the most important, object of defence.

Whether it is easier, harder or impossible to defend our way of life if we were to be occupied, is a very important question which will be discussed in a later chapter.

For the moment I am only concerned to point out that for one reason or another the notion that the enemy must be prevented from occupying the homeland or controlling our sea communications is at present the basic thought in defence policy.

In examining our military defence we must relate it to the nature of the most probable enemy at the time. Just as IT, or what we have been trying to defend, has varied with the circumstances of the day, so has the potential or actual enemy.

In 1914 the enemy was the Kaiser's Germany and what we were trying to defend (plus a certain amount of morality) was what we held. We were not greatly concerned about the danger of having inflicted upon us the German way of life from which our first social services were partly copied.

In 1939 the enemy was Hitler and the Nazi movement, which had managed to secure control of the resources of the German people. By this time—as I have pointed out on page 46—the issue had become less material and more spiritual. We were concerned to prevent our way of life in particular and the democratic way of life in general from being replaced by the anti-semitic, anti-religious, police state totalitarian Nazi system.

Since about the end of World War II the enemy has been Communist Russia. The Communist Party in the Soviet Union, having obtained control of all the resources of that nation, has enormously increased its material power and, if the speeches and actions of the leaders of the Soviet Union are to be taken as a guide, it is their intention by a variety of ways to create conditions in which Communism will be the only permitted way of life all over the world.

It is to prevent this development in world history that we are maintaining in co-operation with other nations large scale military forces.

The price of liberty is continual vigilance and it may be that in years to come the enemy of freedom will be China or perhaps a great African Empire but, for the time being, it is the Soviet Union and this is the ball from which our eyes must not stray.

The Soviet menace is characterized by a number of novel features or, if some of them are not strictly novel, they have been developed by the Russians to an unprecedented degree of magnitude and efficiency.

One of these is the extreme intelligence with which the Russian Communists have understood that—to use my terminology (see page 23)—WAR IS WERRE (the ideological conflict of minds) and not only military operations or violent bodily clashes. They have been further ahead in their thinking on this subject than the democratic statesmen who have been neo-Victorian in this respect. Because of their appreciation of the significance of the ideological struggle or, to use a common phrase, *political warfare*, the Russian leaders have worked out a very nice and, as a rule, an exact and often profitable balance and co-ordination between political and military forces in the operation of their over-all strategy.

The correct defence against political warfare operations, whether directed by Fascists, Nazis or Communists (the cleverest of the bunch of totalitarians), is discussed in Chapter X. Here we are concerned with the military side of the Soviet strategy and the efficacy of our military defence against that part of the Soviet aggression.

Our military defence, as soon as we woke up to the fact after World War II that Marshal Stalin was up to no good, was based on the theory that Russian armed forces might move into areas controlled by democratic governments. Influential Communist parties taking their orders from Moscow existed in France and Italy and it was believed that—as happened in Czechoslovakia—if these Communists succeeded in gaining power either by electoral means or a *coup d'état*—they would be supported by Russian armed force.

The post-war settlement with the states of Hungary, Rumania and Bulgaria included a limitation in their armaments. These conditions were never fulfilled and, as these states with the addition of Poland and Czechoslovakia became Russian satellites, their armed forces were greatly increased. The Soviet Union retained very large forces on a war footing and began actively to increase their strength and efficiency especially in the creation of a large air force, a great fleet of submarines, a large mechanized army and the development of nuclear weapons.

There was a period soon after World War II when it looked as if the Western European economy would collapse into chaos and thus create conditions suitable for a take-over by Communist parties. This peril was averted by massive and generous U.S. economic assistance. A desire on the part of some of the satellite states to take advantage of this offer was promptly squashed by instructions from Moscow. This was an obvious tactical move by the Soviet Union in the economic section of the over-all strategy of the cold war. By 1947-48 there was great tension between the Soviet Union and the Western World and the Western World began to see that if the Soviet Union, whose master at that time was Marshal Stalin, decided to send its armed forces westwards there was nothing of substance to prevent them rapidly reaching the shores of the English Channel and Atlantic Ocean *except* the fact that at that time the Americans, and to a lesser extent the British, had a monopoly of the atom bomb, the fission nuclear weapon first used in 1945 against Japan.

Sir Winston Churchill and others who have access to much unpublished information are on record as stating that the possession by the Allies of this weapon probably saved Western Europe from a Russian invasion.

Whether or not this is true it was obvious that the A-bomb monopoly would not last for long, and a number of incidents involving the betrayal of scientific secrets by western scientists to the Russians indicated that the latter were hard at work catching up with the West in the field of nuclear weapons. In these circumstances the North Atlantic Treaty Organization came into being on 4th April, 1949.

It was originally a military alliance of twelve nations (later fifteen) designed to produce a mobilized shield of conventional forces, sufficiently powerful to hold a Russian-cum-satellite invasion of Western Europe for a period of a month or two whilst the main reserves were mobilized. In short, the thinking in 1949 was in terms of a slightly up to date version of World War II in anticipation of a Russian blitzkrieg westwards.

Mention should also be made of the existence of the non-military Article II in the Treaty which says:

"They (the member states) will contribute toward the further development of peaceful and friendly international relations by strengthening their free institutions, by bringing about a better understanding of the principles upon which these institutions are founded, and by promoting conditions of stability and well-being. They will seek to eliminate conflict in their international economic policies and will encourage economic collaboration between any or all of them."

Up till now (1957) little attention has been paid to Article II, which was introduced into the Treaty in order to facilitate Canadian membership of the club. That Article II has a defence value will be shown in the next chapter and I mention it here both to record its terms and to emphasize that it has not been regarded as a significant fact of our defence.

In 1952 a meeting of the Nato powers was held at Lisbon in order to determine, in the light of the Soviet Union's strength in conventional forces, what should be the size of the Nato forces. The military experts advised that their requirements were: "Approximately 50 divisions in combat readiness and 4,000 operational aircraft in Western Europe."

At the time the West German Republic was not regarded as a potential member of Nato. It seemed to me: (a) that the electorates of the member states would refuse to make the sacrifices required to maintain forces of this size, and (b) that to exclude the West Germans from the calculations of the potential available for the physical defence of Western Europe was to still further increase the immense difficulties of the task.

It would be superfluous to record the story of Nato in any detail during the years 1951 to 1957. The fact is that by 1957 the military position of the West in terms of conventional weapons had steadily deteriorated relative to that of the Soviet Union.

The following extracts from successive British White Papers on Defence illustrate developments.

1951. "(There is) an urgent need to strengthen the defences of the free world. H.M.G. has decided to increase and accelerate their defence preparations . . . the total strength of the armed forces will by April 1952 reach 800,000 men as compared with 682,000 in the last White Paper on defence . . . expenditure on production for the Services in 1951-52 will be more than double the rate for the current year . . . by 1953-54 it should be more than four times as great . . . the total defence budget for 1951-54 may be £4,700 million . . . though the burden will be heavy, it is not more than we can bear . . . this (is) a national effort to make ourselves strong enough to deter any attack upon our freedom and our way of life."

1952. This statement was an explanation of why there had been delays in implementing the 1951 programme. It was devoid of strategical or tactical thought except that it contained an announcement that in order "to combat the risk of invasion" it had been decided to re-establish the Home Guard and that "numerous training schools" had been told to "acquire a

combatant value". The statement added that "this development has greatly increased our ability to defend ourselves
against attack".[1]

1953. The introduction explained why the programme must
be reduced. "Our objectives have not changed; it is the means
of achieving them and the rate at which we can progress . . . to
which the Government has given much close attention."

1954. "Provided that our defence effort is maintained and
that we continue to conduct our diplomacy with patience and
resolution, it is the Government's view that the continuation
for a long period of the present state of cold war is now more
likely than the outbreak of a major war at any particular date
. . . the Government propose to continue the policy fore-
shadowed last year and for the next few years to maintain our
defence effort at the maximum which our economic capabilities permit." This statement on defence was noteworthy for its
remarks about the "broken-backed war" and that "if, by some
miscalculation in Communist policy or by deliberate design,
a global war were forced upon us, it must be assumed that
atomic weapons would be used by both sides."

"The principal aims of the country's defence programme"
were "briefly expressed" as follows:

"First we must maintain our resistance to world Communism and to Communist adventures and discharge our
peacetime obligations overseas. Secondly, we must with our
allies, build up the most effective possible deterrent against a
major aggression which would lead to global war. Thirdly, we
must do all we can, within the limits of our resources to be
prepared to meet such an aggression should our efforts to
prevent it fail."

The statement recorded the theory that "our active forces
must be able to withstand the initial shock. Our reserve force
must be capable of rapid mobilization behind the shield . . .
and be ready to perform their combat tasks at the earliest
possible moment." "Civil Defence is an essential, integral and
continuing part of our defence preparation for any future war."

---

[1] I rate this one of the most optimistic remarks ever made in the name of
defence. S.K-H.

1955. "Overshadowing all else in the year 1954 has been the emergence of the thermo-nuclear bomb. This has had, and will continue to have, far reaching effects on the defence policy of the U.K." After describing the effects of an H-bomb, the statement continued "Public morale would be severely tested. It would be a struggle for survival of the grimmest kind." For the first time in these statements we see a reference to "other" means of defence in the sentence "The deterrent to aggression does not consist in military strength alone. The political unity and resolution and the economic strength of the free world must be maintained."

The statement included long passages on the cold war and the deterrent, and on the first subject it made the important remark: "Political unity and armed strength would be of little value *if the will of the free peoples to maintain, and if necessary defend their independence and way of life were in doubt*"[1] and the impression from the passage on the deterrent is that the centre of gravity of defence had shifted to the deterrent. But one also reads in paragraphs 22 and 23 the clear statement that as we are and must remain outnumbered in conventional forces: "With their aid (nuclear weapons) and with the German contribution we can adopt a forward strategy on the ground in Europe and so defend the Continent, instead of contemplating again the grim process of liberation. If we do not use the full weight of our nuclear power, Europe can hardly be protected from invasion and occupation . . . the consciences of civilized nations must naturally recoil from the prospect of using nuclear weapons. Nevertheless, in the last resort, most of us must feel *that determination to face the threat of physical devastation, even on the immense scale which must now be foreseen, is manifestly preferable, to an attitude of subservience to militant Communism with the national and individual humiliation that this would inevitably bring.*"

1956. This statement was significant because it elaborated in greater detail than ever before the political and strategic factors in our defence policy as seen by H.M.G. Under the political heading we read:

"There is no change in Soviet long-term policy which fundamentally aims at world domination. The Soviet Government continue to believe in their right, indeed in their mission,

[1] Italics mine in this chapter.

to impose political and economic systems on other nations and to withhold from them the right to choose their own future . . . their policies are openly directed to achieving this end (world domination). . . . The aim of the democracies is to establish peace and prosperity within which the peoples of the world can develop their lives in freedom. The military forces of the democracies must be designed to support this aim . . . it therefore remains necessary for the western powers to hold their own in the world by their defensive strength *until such time as a true understanding of western policies can make its impact on the Soviet people.*"

This statement also announced that the manpower in the forces would be reduced to 700,000 by March 1958.[1]

This defence review had "regard to probable developments over the next seven years".

1957. "The time has now come to revise not merely the size *but the whole character of the defence plan.* The Communist threat remains, but *its nature has changed* and it is now evident that on both military and economic grounds, it is necessary to make a fresh appreciation of the problem and to adopt a new approach to it." The statement was silent as to how the nature of the Communist threat (which remains) has changed. This is a very extraordinary omission as I pointed out in Chapter I, p. 37.

As a supplement to the 1957 White Paper one should note the Minister of Defence's statement in Australia in August 1957 in which he went a great deal further in stating Government policy than anything which had been said in debate in the Commons. Mr. Sandys said that, notwithstanding the merits of the latest type of British fighter, some enemy bombers would get through with hydrogen bombs; then he said: "*That is why we have taken a very bold step in deciding not to do the impossible. We decided not to defend the whole country, but to defend only our bomber bases. I must pay tribute to the people of Great Britain for the readiness with which they have accepted these harsh but inescapable facts.*" ▬

This statement is the latest pronouncement available at the moment of writing and should be considered carefully by every citizen, even if he is not quite clear as to how he has earned the tribute paid to him by Mr. Sandys. For this statement could be reworded as follows, without, as I see it, altering its meaning:

[1] cf. the 1951 Statement.

"Our defences will be concentrated on defending against sudden attack our airfields from which retaliatory action will take place. We cannot defend the great cities, but you may rest assured that whilst you are being destroyed, or at any rate very shortly afterwards, a like fate will be the lot of millions of Russians. Thank you for accepting this harsh fact, but we have no other suggestion to make to you." The American public may not know it, but they are in the same embarrassing posture, and likely to be in it for a long time.

A close study of the succession of White Papers, from which extracts have been reproduced, leads to some conclusions. They are that defence thinking has been almost completely confined to the military sphere. From time to time, like gleams of sunlight in a dark and stormy sky, there is a sentence or two indicating that more comprehensive thinking about defence has inspired the mind of the author of the paper. There is a reference, for example, in 1955 to "our way of life" as being an object of defence, but it is hard to find any remark in these documents suggesting that there is any alternative to military force as a means of defence. In 1956 we read that we must hope for a day when "a true understanding of western policies can make its impact on the Soviet people". But immediately preceding this sagacious remark is the statement that until such time as the Soviet people are in this desirable frame of mind the West must rely on its "defensive strength".

Bearing in mind the premise of the White Papers that defence means military defence, it is unreasonable to criticize them for this narrow approach. It is as if the B.M.A. were to publish a paper on orthodox medical practices in relation to health and then be blamed for not considering unorthodox methods such as faith healing.

Since the White Papers stick to their brief, they inevitably reveal the confusion of thought and changes of policy which culminate in the statement made by a Minister of Defence (and an able one) that the Government has taken "the *very bold step* in deciding *not to do the impossible*".

Let us now return, after this examination of military defence policy, to the situation which this policy has produced in the military sphere.

II

The conventional military position of Nato *vis-à-vis* the Soviet Union in 1957 was approximately as follows:

The Soviet Union was believed to have approximately 70 divisions exclusive of reserves, 2,000 bomber aircraft, 4,000 fighter aircraft and between 400 and 450 submarines, by far the largest submarine force ever known to naval history.[1]

The Nato Supreme Commander could theoretically call on the services of about 15 divisions but, owing to the Algerian rebellion most of the French Army was in N. Africa, and only 3 out of a target figure of 12 German divisions were on the ground; these were partially trained. In the air the Nato forces were probably about equal in strength to those of the Soviet Union. Particulars of the Nato anti-submarine forces were difficult to obtain but, in the light of the experience of dealing with a far smaller number of U-boats during World War II, an experience which taxed the resources of the Allies to the utmost, the scale of defence required against 400 (plus) Russian submarines is enormous. I should be astonished to learn that the Board of Admiralty have the slightest hope of persuading any government to authorize the gigantic naval estimates which would be necessary to ensure with reasonable certainty that the activities of this enormous Soviet submarine fleet could be mastered, especially as the Russian blockade of Britain would be accompanied by intense aerial activity.

My guess about the inadequacy of our naval defences had hardly been committed to paper when Admiral Sir John Eccles said, on 27th September, 1957: "We have not got anything like enough forces with which to carry out our primary task, either in the air, under the sea or on the sea. We are desperately short. . . . I say as a professional man with over 40 years experience I cannot carry out my task as given to me at the moment without more forces . . . to enter a war with the forces at my disposal . . . (would be) running a very, very grave risk." He added that the underwater threat had increased to a much greater extent than the defences' capability. The Admiral's remarks were strongly supported by his Air

---

[1] At the outbreak of the 1939-45 War the German Navy had about 50 submarines in operation.

Force colleague, Air Marshal Sir Bryan Reynolds. These officers are the Joint Commanders Eastern Atlantic. All in all, and confining our attention for the moment to conventional weapons, the Nato forces in 1957 were greatly inferior to those of the Soviet Union and probably more so than at any time in the history of Nato.

This inferiority being known to all, political leaders had to adapt policies to means and find some other justification for Nato to replace its original object, which as mentioned earlier had been to have sufficient conventional forces on the ground in Western Europe, in the skies and on the ocean to hold a Russian invasion and ultimately break it with a counter-attack. When it became clear that this purpose had not been achieved the trip-wire theory became popular. This school of thought argued that Nato conventional forces should be regarded as being more or less of a token character or trip-wire which, if overwhelmed by superior Russian forces, would automatically bring into action the American strategic airforce armed with nuclear weapons.

The trip-wire theory was not in favour for long probably because the general staffs pointed out that, if carried to its logical conclusion, conventional forces could be reduced to a line of sentries armed with rifles.

It was replaced by the tactical atomic shield theory, the supporters of this idea argued as follows:

"It is true that in terms of man-power, tanks and perhaps tactical aircraft, Nato forces are inferior. But if our numerically inferior forces are armed with tactical nuclear weapons their fire power can be enormously increased and the 'Russian masses' may become a handicap instead of an advantage to the enemy."

The theory of the tactical atomic shield was and is an attempt to get back to the idea, implicit in the original formation of Nato, that the free world must have enough military strength to hold and repel a Russian attack on Western Europe.

The White Paper on Defence 1957 said: "The frontiers of the free world, particularly in Europe, must be firmly defended

OUR MILITARY DEFENCE 91

on the ground" (para 20), and went on, "Britain must provide
her fair share of the armed forces needed for this purpose"
(para 21).

There was no mention in the White Paper of what size these
armed forces must be, but we know from other sources as well
as one's common sense that an absolute minimum of 30
divisions ready for action is required. My own opinion for
technical reasons conncected with the need to be able to stage a
counter-offensive into the satellite states, is that 50 divisions is
a more realistic figure.

The population and resources of the Nato countries are such
that 50 divisions with appropriate tactical aircraft is a force
within the capacity of these countries to produce and maintain
if the governments and peoples thought it worth while to make
the effort. It seems that they do not, and nowhere is this more
evident than in the United Kingdom. This—apart from one's
general knowledge of public opinion and the widespread
dislike of conscription and increased taxation—is shown by
paras 22 and 23 of the White Paper on Defence 1957.

For, having stated in para 21 that Britain must bear her
"fair" share, the next two paragraphs explained that Britain's
forces on the Continent will be reduced from about 77,000 men
to 64,000 men within 12 months, and by more later on, whilst
the second tactical airforce in Germany will be cut by 50 per
cent. This reduction to be offset by providing some of the
squadrons with nuclear bombs. The reduced army will have
"atomic rocket artillery".

There was also the rather odd statement that this reduction
will be accompanied by a re-organization which "will increase
the proportion of fighting units". This seems to indicate care-
lessness up to date.

These reductions by the British Government (which,
determined to economize on armaments, unilaterally decided
what its "fair" share should be), spread dismay and alarm on
the Continent.

It will be surprising if the Nato command does not find
that other countries give thought to what their "fair" share
should be, and it will be more surprising if it is not less than
it is at present! Both the trip-wire theory of the function of
Nato and the tactical atomic shield idea, which seem to be

fashionable at the moment of writing, aroused misgiving amongst the Continental members of Nato who felt in the trip-wire theory they would be over-run and have to await liberation and in the shield idea that the tactical atomic weapons would be falling on their homelands.

Indeed in all thinking on defence against Russia by military means one can distinguish three modes of thought. (*a*) The American and Canadian, (*b*) the British, and (*c*) the Continental. Each mental climate is conditioned by the distance of the homeland from the point of impact of the two belligerents.

Up till now I have limited discussion to the military organization of Nato, but this does not stand alone. It is buttressed by the American strategic air command which is *not* part of Nato. Before discussing the role of this formation it should be recorded that, notwithstanding the wide gap which exists between Nato as it was planned and Nato as it is, the Nato soldiers, sailors and airmen have done a remarkable job with the means at their disposal. In joint training and planning and in the creation of common services, i.e. air-fields, lines of communication, etc., there has been achieved a degree of co-operation at the technical level between nationals of many states which has hitherto rarely been attained in allied military operations and never in so-called peacetime.

III

If Nato collapsed the U.S.A. strategic airforce would remain. It consists of the most powerful force of bombers in the world and is equipped with nuclear weapons. It is an independent command controlled from Omaha in the U.S.A. and maintained at an astonishingly high degree of readiness. It operates from bases in the U.S.A., in the North polar regions, in Britain, Spain, North Africa and Arabia. By the use of tanker planes its latest bomber the B58 can reach all parts of the Soviet Union, and it has been officially stated that all the targets have been pre-selected so that at very short notice the Soviet Union could be heavily saturated with nuclear bombs. I have been told on good authority that some of its planes, fully armed, are always in the air.[1] This is certainly true of its aerial radar stations.

[1] This was officially confirmed in December 1957.

Although the Soviet Union is believed to have caught up in quality with the American jet bombers and may be on the point of exceeding them in quantity, the Americans have the edge on the Russians for the time being because the American bases are closer to Russian targets than the Russian bases are to American targets such as New York and Chicago.

This is not an advantage enjoyed by Britain. On the contrary a great many Russian targets are further from British bases in the U.K. than London, Liverpool, Glasgow, etc., are from Russian bases.

Why have the Russians built such an enormous fleet of submarines? The reason seems likely to be the perfectly sensible one of being able to disrupt sea communications between N. America and Europe. This plan made particular sense in the days when Nato was pictured as a force sufficiently powerful (without nuclear weapons) to hold a Russian conventional offensive for a period of two or three months. It was assumed in those far-off days—about six years ago!—that, during this period, the reserve divisions of the Nato powers would be mobilized and enter the battle in a comforting and increasing stream.

Some people think that the present purpose of the large Russian submarine fleet is that of providing a large number of mobile concealed stations from which to project nuclear weapons on to the U.S.A. This would effectively counter the disadvantage the Russians are temporarily enduring by being surrounded at distances of from 2,000-5,000 miles by the bases of the American strategic bombing force.

This theory makes a good story, but guided missiles and their launching apparatus are at present (1957) large and heavy units and I should be astonished to learn that the Russian submarine fleet could be fitted to carry and launch the big ones.[1] More probable reasons for the large fleet are:

(a) The Russians made a mistake in 1945 and planned for World War III too much in terms of World War II.

(b) They may think (and be right) that until one side is near defeat nuclear weapons will not be used and, in a

[1] But in September 1957 the American Commander of the 6th Fleet declared he had submarines capable of launching missiles.

non-nuclear war, they will exercise command of the sea
by submarines.

(c) They foresee submarines using guided tactical nuclear
weapons and are planning for this development by
training a large number of officers and men in submarine warfare.

But technical advances are taking place so rapidly that it
would be imprudent not to visualize atomic powered submarines of large displacement armed with guided missiles.

The master weapon of the lot, the Queen of Destruction, is
the ICBM (the Intercontinental Ballistic Missile); it does not
yet exist in production, but millions are being spent by the
U.S.A. and Russia on its development and it may be operational by 1963, if not earlier.

The above paragraph was out of date within a week of being
written, when the Russians announced the first successful
flight of an ICBM and soon afterwards startled the world with
their satellite. I have let the paragraph stand but perhaps the
date 1963 should have three years lopped off it.

Some formidable technical problems have yet to be solved.
The Intercontinental Missile carrying an H-bomb of megaton
proportions will probably travel to a height of about 600 miles
and at a speed of Mach 20, i.e. in the region of 14,000 miles
an hour. In August 1957 the Russians claimed this result.

This kind of thing makes the V2's which fell on London in
1945 seem like Chinese fire-crackers lobbed over the garden
wall. It has been officially estimated that a dozen large H-
bombs would "inflict widespread devastation" on Great Britain
and that "there is at present no means of providing adequate
protection for the people of this country against the consequences of an attack by nuclear weapons".[1] From such
studies as I have made of the data available it is my personal
conviction that the phrase "widespread devastation" is official
English for "a smoking radio-active charnel house". Although
the Intercontinental Missile is not yet what an American
general described as "operational hardware" its older brother,
the Intermediate Range B.M., is just passing out of the experimental stage and seems to be in production in the Soviet Union.

[1] Defence Paper 1957, para 12.

It has a range of 1,500 miles and carries the H-bomb to the target at the relatively slow speed of about 2,000-3,000 miles per hour.

Its significance to Britain is considerable because we are now, or very shortly will be, within striking range of the Inter-mediate Missile launched from Russian bases. It will take about 25 minutes for this rocket to travel from Leningrad to London. The short-range guided missile with a range of a few hundred miles is almost a conventional weapon.

According to Press reports on 27th September, 1957 the Midland Regional Director of Civil Defence, speaking to a national conference of industrial civil defence officers, said that in the event of an atomic attack it was the Government's official view that we should get five minutes' warning. He also said that the Government was planning, should another war break out, to evacuate 40 to 45 per cent of the population of the highly industrialized areas leaving only the able-bodied men and childless women![1] I find it impossible to take seriously these vague plans for enormous evacuations, although I believe that if it appeared that there was a serious risk of nuclear attack developing there would be an immense and chaotic unofficial evacuation of large cities. This is one of the risks which makes it so difficult for any government to take pre-cautionary measures—such as they are—in the nuclear age comparable to the various stages of mobilization in the pre-nuclear age.

Furthermore there is a new defence problem which seems to have escaped attention. In 1957 there was an accident at the Windscale atomic energy plant which caused the escape of injurious radio-active substances. Millions of pounds are now being invested in the construction of atomic power stations in many parts of Great Britain. They are enormous fixed instal-lations whose precise distance and bearing from rocket-firing bases in the Soviet Union can be exactly computed. What would happen if one or more of these vast structures, housing within their massive protecting walls immense lethal forces, were struck by an H-bomb or even rocked on their foundations by an H-bomb explosion within 10 miles of their site? If an

[1] I am in some doubt as to how the wives of the able-bodied men would react to this part of our defence plan. S.K.-H.

atomic power station in the West of Britain was disintegrated with a prevailing south-west wind, might not 30 per cent of the country be contaminated? According to the Russian statements their ICBM was accurate to within 6 to 12 miles of the target.

Something must now be said about so-called tactical nuclear weapons.

We have seen that the ability to produce small nuclear weapons—the so-called tactical weapon—has been used as an excuse or an argument to justify reduction in conventional weapons. My information is that at this time (1957) the baby of the tactical nuclear weapon is a shell which can be discharged from a mortar and has a radius of destruction of about 1,000 yards. From this little bang one moves up to a nuclear bomb able to be carried in one aircraft (soon to be replaced by rockets) which, in the words of a senior U.S.A.F. officer, has an explosive force equal to all the explosives dropped on Germany in World War II.

The tactical weapon seems to have exceedingly dangerous possibilities. Suppose a clash occurs in Europe and begins conventionally. It has now become conventional to use tactical nuclear weapons. Nato—or the American forces therein—has got them and will use them. It is reasonable to suppose that the enemy will retaliate in kind and with larger tactical nuclear weapons. It will only be of historic interest which side is the first to counter an atomic kiloton bomb with an H-bomb in the megaton range. Everything will have remained strictly tactical.

Much has been written and said by members of a school of thought who believe that it is possible to have limited nuclear wars. The most famous spokesman of this doctrine is an American, Mr. H. A. Kissinger, whose book *Nuclear Weapons and Foreign Policy* was widely discussed.

This school of thought, who sometimes refer to their idea as that of the graduated deterrent, start from the sound basis that if the only method we have of using violence in defence is that of all-out nuclear war, which is suicidal, we shall never use it first. Therefore the Russians will be able to make successive aggressions, which will not be sufficiently monstrous to call for an all-out nuclear attack. I agree with this and hold the view it is most unlikely that the West will ever launch an H-bomb attack except in retaliation for one they have endured. The limited war school of thought then proceed to argue that a kind of gentleman's agreement must be worked out and known to exist in advance, which will limit the war. It is suggested, for example, that each side is to treat the other's strategic air base as a "sanctuary" immune from attack and only military installations within the battle zone (whatever that may be supposed to be) are to be bombed. I believe such ideas to be fallacious and their authors are bogged down in a desperate attempt to square the circle. For what they are trying to do is not only to confine nuclear energy for military purposes into the strait-jacket of conventional war, but even restrict that strait-jacket and revive the formal rules of war which had some validity in some wars of the Middle Ages and the pre-total war era. They may not know it, but they are trying to conventional-ize nuclear energy for military purposes; one might as well endeavour to sanctify the Devil. You either use him or you don't! You cannot enlist him in the firm as a sleeping partner or technical adviser.

There is something else to be said about the tactical nuclear weapon—and I owe this thought to an interjection made at a meeting by a stranger—it is that, even if in certain circum-stances the tactical nuclear weapon can be limited in space, *it cannot be limited in time*. The radio-active consequences of nuclear war and weapon tests on future generations through harmful mutations, about which we know little (but none of which is nice), are not limited.

IV

I will now consider the deterrent; the Great Deterrent.

Both sides have got H-bombs, and I might as well try to keep this book up-to-date by assuming that the Interconti-nental Ballistic Missile is available. If you feel this is cheating, then for the very large missile substitute the jet bomber forces of American B58's, British Valiants and Vulcans and Russian Bisons and the medium range missile.

The theory of the deterrent as expounded by the free world runs as follows:

D

"The Russians have been told that any major act of aggression on their side, and in particular a nuclear attack by them on us, would be followed by instant and massive nuclear retaliation. If therefore the Russians wish to commit suicide this is the way to do it."

That—put I hope with fairness and moderation—is our official position. I cannot help wondering whether unofficially the free world leaders say under their breath: "We hope to goodness the Russians believe this."

Do they?[1] I hope we shall never have to find out by practical experiment. But some questions must be asked.

(a) Is it not true, or at any rate highly probable, that the free world will *not* be the first to drop an H-bomb? Apart from one's inner sense of what democracies do and do not do and the unlikelihood (I hope) that any H-bomb would be dropped by the U.S.A. or Britain without mutual consultation[2]—all of which takes time—the White Paper 1957 says that so far as Britain is concerned "the only safeguard against major aggression is *the power to threaten retaliation with nuclear weapons*" (italics mine). It also writes of "the initial nuclear bombardment and *counter-bombardment*" (para 24). Although it is not clearly stated who is to make the initial bombardment, I believe it unlikely that the White Paper supposes it to be ourselves. If I have misread the White Paper, and it means we are to take the initiative, what are we to make of the further statement that: "It may well be (the two bombardments) would be so crippling as to bring the war to an end within a few weeks or even days."

(b) If it is true or probable that we shall not initiate H-bomb war, then is there not a danger that the Russians may also reach this conclusion? If *they* are prepared to initiate it (and we take it for granted that they will not be inhibited by moral scruples), is there not a danger that they will argue something

[1] Many recent quotations could be cited from Khrushchev and Russian marshals intimating they are satisfied that, though all-out nuclear war would be highly destructive, the Soviet Union would survive and the West would not. One would expect them to *say* this sort of thing and no one can be sure whether or not their appreciation of a major nuclear war is correct or false, but my hunch is that they do believe what they say.

[2] H.M.G. has received an undertaking from the U.S. that American aircraft carrying H-bombs based in East Anglia will not be used without British permission.

as follows: "We shall—perhaps after a conventional opening—suddenly launch a nuclear attack on the U.S.A. and the United Kingdom. In the era of Intercontinental Missiles the enemy will have a few minutes of warning that the missiles have been launched. Even to-day the British might have only a few minutes' warning by radar that the missiles are en route. It is inconceivable that by any method of organization in a democracy anyone can order a counter-bombardment in five minutes. If nothing happens during those minutes much of the United Kingdom will be pulverized and there may be no counter-attack or only a partial one."

In connection with this hypothesis, what arrangements do exist or could be imagined to exist in Britain to enable a counter nuclear bombardment to be launched on the sole basis of radar evidence (if radar can deal with ICBM's) that missiles ex-Russia are in the stratosphere?[1]

The only arrangement I can conceive is that *after* the nuclear missiles have fallen, some survivors in some deep shelter will endeavour to set the counter-bombardment in motion if its organization has not been destroyed. And, even should it be possible to launch a blow of revenge, what good will that do if we are already destroyed?

Does not the same argument apply to the U.S.A.-Soviet situation?

Probably not at the moment because the U.S.A. is not at present (1957) quite so open to sudden attack as is the U.K. But it will apply to the U.S.A. as soon as the ICBM is developed.

(c) But, granted that under (b) above, the Russians may lean on that argument, are they not also likely to feel that, even if they knock out Britain in the way described, there will be instant retaliation from the U.S.A.?

That is the theory but how sure are we that there is and always will be unanimity of thought between London and Washington as to when an H-bomb is to be dropped? Are we sure that each country is committed irrevocably to join the

---

[1] According to a report presented to W.E.U. by Lord Stonehaven, M.A.: "An electronic computer used to intercept an attacking guided missile would have to perform nearly 3,000 calculations, feed the information to the defending missile and guide it to the target in a little over 2 minutes." *Manchester Guardian*, 14th October, 1957.

other in nuclear war irrespective of how and why each country becomes involved in hostilities? Why does the British Government keep on saying that Britain *must* have H-bombs so as to preserve its political independence *vis-à-vis* the U.S.A.?

Reflections of this nature have been engaging the attention of the leaders of the West and one of them, a very intelligent man of wide experience, has spoken out on this matter. I refer to some remarks made by Mr. Lester B. Pearson. He wrote:[1]

"Who decides that all-out aggression has begun? Who decides when to press the button which brings about air retaliation through nuclear strategic bombing? Certainly not any Nato command or council in so far as the U.S. strategic airforce is concerned. This problem of such decisive importance remains to be solved . . . an attempt to force a solution would be unwise because it would not be likely to result in agreed and clear-cut decisions and might well result in dissensions and trouble inside the alliance."

Since the Russians can read and write as well as encircle us with artificial satellites, the above passage will be known to them. Is it fanciful to suppose that Khrushchev must be thinking: "They talk about the Great Deterrent and yet they know that we know that for fear of falling out amongst themselves they dare not even try to solve the problem of who presses the button and when? I do not feel very deterred."

V

The purpose of this chapter has been to examine our military defence arrangements and consider to what extent they are likely to be effective against large-scale Russian military aggression against the institutions of our way of life, arrangements which are epitomized in the deterrent of the H-bomb.

It is interesting to reflect that in relying on the deterrent we are (maybe unconsciously) operating in the field of ideas. We are relying on a belief, or wishful hope, that if we possess H-bombs—or even if we do not, but are sure the Russians believe we have them—this will produce a thought in the minds of the

[1] In *Western World*, September 1957.

Russian leaders which can be summed up as: "It (our con-templated aggression) is not worth the consequences."

It is said officially that however intense and elaborate physical defences against enemy bombers may be, a percentage of them will get through. In other words "Nothing is 100 per cent sure". The same observation applies to our estimate of what is going on in the minds of the Russian leaders. We have no grounds whatsoever for being *sure* that the fear of a counter-bombardment is *the* restraining influence on Russian minds contemplating military aggression. It is impossible to be *sure* about anything (with one exception) in this baffling exercise in international thought-reading. A distinguished member of the Labour Party told me that he objected to my idea of an enquiry into the possible value of non-violent resistance as a basis of defence strategy, because the mere fact of a few people round a table in Britain discussing the pros and cons of N.V.R. as a defence strategy might cause the Russians to think: "These British are not 100 per cent sound on the obvious value of their deterrent."

My comment was that I did not think he could have the faith he claimed to have in the unassailable character of the deterrent argument if he feared the effect upon its psychological value of an intellectual exercise on the subject of a possible alternative. "Would you feel happier," I asked, "if the enquiry were labelled Most Secret?"

An interesting point in connection with the deterrent which I have not seen dealt with in public is this:

I assume our leaders are not misleading either us or the Russians when they say that we can blast Russia to pieces, otherwise we are founding our policy on a terribly dangerous bluff. The deterrent depends upon the Soviet leaders *being sure* it is not a bluff.

Therefore part of the deterrent policy should be an invitation to the Russians to attend our tests and see with their own eyes how terrible our bombs can be. Indeed if the Russians have got H-bombs and, without further scientific research, can already produce the largest explosion of any possible use in military operations, and their problem is now one of stock-piling, it is for consideration whether we should not offer to exchange a 20 megaton bomb and thus make quite sure that each side knows without doubt what each can do to the other, and how horrible it would be.

If this proposal to modify the conventional practice of keeping weapons secret to the needs of a policy based on the deterrent is too radical, I offer the following suggestion:

The Americans have stated that progress is being made with a clean bomb, i.e. non-radio-active fall-out. Surely the scientific information connected with this development should be passed forthwith to Moscow. I see no military advantage to us in a state of affairs in which in nuclear war we drop clean bombs and receive dirty ones. The only argument against the passing of this information is that if the Russians only have dirty bombs they might not use them because of the uncertain consequences of the fall-out. I do not attach importance to this thought.

I wrote just now that there was only one aspect of this whole question about which I thought we could be sure we knew the truth, the whole truth and nothing but the truth. What we know for a fact is this:

That in this year of grace 1957 the main strategy of defence of the U.K. is based on the threat to use a weapon (the H-bomb) which we have publicly admitted would—if ever used—cause the destruction of what we are trying to defend. And this is true, whether or not you agree with my belief that what we are trying to defend is our way of life or whether you prefer the traditional notion that we are only trying to defend our material possessions.

Never threaten what you cannot or will not be sure to perform, is a sound maxim in life.

But—the deterrent school of thought will reply: "We can and we do intend to carry out our threats."

They must reflect that they have no right to use the word WE, if by that word they mean any body of men who represent the nation. As Mr. Bevan pointed out in a speech in June 1957,[1] the H-bomb business makes it impossible to suppose that Parliament would have time to decide anything. It is very unlikely the Cabinet would be in any better shape and the

[1] In September 1957 Mr. Bevan, who had previously seemed to be against Britain having H-bombs, fell into line with the official Labour attitude that we must have the Bomb.

discussion would have to be very brief, even if Mr. Bevan were in office.

The word WE in practice means (if we—you and I—are prepared to give them the necessary power) two men acting jointly or severally, i.e. the President of the U.S.A. and the Prime Minister of Great Britain.

A heavy addition to the responsibilities of these two over-worked gentlemen and one which, as I shall suggest in Chapter IX, we might usefully relieve our man.

VI

It may help the reader, as it has certainly helped me, if I try to relate some of the reflections set forth in this chapter to a possible episode or conceivable case of aggression:

Let us suppose that there is a rising of the people in East Germany. The East German government calls for help from the Russians who exercise military force. The military forces suppressing the revolt declare that it is being organized from West Berlin (a possible truth) and that, in order to control East Berlin, they must occupy West Berlin. They advance into West Berlin with four mechanized divisions and tactical air-craft. Perhaps they put down an airborne division into West Berlin. They say to the small allied force: "Keep out of the way", or: "You had better evacuate yourselves to West Germany under safe conduct."

What happens next? Here are some possibilities. Assuming agreement between Paris, London and Washington, the allied troops in Berlin (1) retire, or (2) die to the last man. I doubt whether the Allied Commander in Berlin has precise instruction what he is to do. But would there be agreement amongst the Allies? Do not forget what Mr. Pearson has told us on page 100.

As soon as Russian troop movements are reported, the scrambled telephone talks begin between Washington-Paris-London, and, one may be sure, Bonn would expect to be consulted.

Is this a "major act of aggression?" It looks like it even though the Russians are saying: "The occupation is temporary and only to put down illegal activities against the lawful govern-ment of East Germany." Do the U.S.A. and Britain, without warning of any kind, open up a nuclear attack on Russia? I should not think so. Does the U.S.A. announce: "If West Berlin is not evacuated within 6 hours (or 12 hours) we will blast Russia?" Would the Russian reply to this be to blast the U.S.A. and Britain at zero plus 5 hours (or 11 hours) without warning?

What will people be doing in London, New York, Chicago and other large centres when this situation arises? Might there not be a panic evacuation and scenes of indescribable chaos?

Suppose the British Cabinet were simply told by the Americans (with more courtesy than we showed to them over Suez); "We tell you that we intend to have a show-down over this Berlin business. We think we can call their bluff and, if we cannot, we can hurt them more than they can hurt us." What would the Cabinet do?

Would it say to Washington: "We cannot have Britain destroyed by Intermediate Range Missiles. We are telling the Russians your nuclear bombers cannot take off from Britain and we will not drop nuclear bombs on Russia if they do not drop any on us"? Or would we say: "Britain is with you to the last heap of radio-active ashes. If you survive, remember us in the history books." I suggest we can all imagine what the French will be saying, and the Asian Dominions would certainly leave the Commonwealth without delay and loudly trumpet their neutrality.

Another guess—and I admit my guess is no better than yours —is that when the news came through that West Berlin had been seized, the Allies would seek a way out of their hideous dilemma by summoning an emergency meeting of the Security Council where Russia would exercise the veto. "Law and Order" would be restored in East Germany whilst the debate was taking place.

I will go out on a limb and risk being branded as a coward and an appeaser by saying that in the circumstance I have tried to imagine, the governments of the democratic countries will *not* risk starting up a nuclear war and that, if given a chance to express an opinion, a very small proportion of the people of the free world would decide that an illegal Russian occupation of Berlin should lead to the destruction of civilization. I fear the Russians might reach the same conclusion.

Russian action of this kind would be aggression of a serious character and, if they got away with it, they would be tempted to repeat the performance. They might, for example, if circumstances were favourable, renew their attempts to bring Greece into their orbit by a mixture of internal dissension and external Russian aid.

If the Russians got away with it in the case mentioned above, what was missing? What should we have lacked? The answer is: Adequate conventional force. If the Russians knew that in the event of their seizing West Berlin a powerful Nato conventional force would back up an ultimatum to withdraw, they might hesitate. In the last resort the Nato force, if powerful enough, could drive them out of Berlin, and lay the onus on the Russians of using nuclear weapons.

We are now back to the conception of conventional war which was becoming so destructive through traditional operational methods by 1945 that its merits were dubious, but not so destructive that it had become suicidal folly. Indeed, if looked at in a cold-blooded way and in long-term historical perspective, the destruction wrought by conventional military operations by 1945 and the miseries it inflicted on Germany forced this virile nation to re-build its cities and work so hard to live, that by 1957 their prosperity was an international embarrassment. But as things are in 1957 we have not got conventional weapons of sufficient strength to deny the capture of West Berlin to the Russians, or retake it if it were lost.

But we have got Nato and we pretend that our set-up there of conventional forces plus tactical nuclear weapons is a defence for Europe.

Let us therefore suppose that in the case we have imagined the Russians seize West Berlin and both sides declare they will not use the H-bomb.

Nevertheless it is felt in London and Washington that, if the Russians get away with this, what is the object of having Nato? Therefore a conventional war begins. This now begins to look like the limited war discussed on page 96. This school of thought would be saying in broadcasts and articles: "Do not worry too much; remember the Korean example, where in their own interests both sides observed certain conventions, viz. the U.N. forces never bombed the enemy aerodromes

beyond the Yalu River because it was felt this would bring
China into the war and so risk starting up a world war and
probably a nuclear one, whilst the N. Koreans never bombed
our ports because if they had done so we should have had to
retaliate on their aerodromes in China."

This school of thought would therefore argue in the Berlin
case we are discussing that there might be a limited conventional war. Unfortunately this argument is sunk on the rock of
tactical nuclear weapons. The Russians might well not be the
first to use nuclear weapons; they would not need to do so as
their mechanized divisions poured westwards, but we have *got*
to use tactical nuclear weapons from the start in order to
compensate for the Russian masses.[1] We have announced
officially that we shall do so. The Russian general staff would
not allow its troops to be subjected to nuclear attack without
retaliating in kind. The retaliation might be limited in the first
instance to an atomic bomb(s) on Antwerp, one of the main
bases of the Nato forces. This would call for correspondingly
heavy stuff on the main Soviet bases. The enemy would then
give serious consideration to getting rid of Britain with a
dozen H-bombs. This would mean a full-scale nuclear war.

I have dealt with the case of the West Berlin seizure in terms
of limited war in order to illustrate why those who back this
theory (i.e. that the H-bomb deterrent creates a framework
in which limited wars can be conducted) overlook the fact, the
truly appalling fact, that tactical nuclear weapons are now
conventional weapons.

The West Berlin case is a glance into the future, but this is
such an important matter that I will illustrate it with an
example of what might have been. Consider the Suez episode
and exclude from it all issues of domestic controversy. Strategically the dilemma of the British Government was that it was
trying to fight a limited war of a novel character. It was trying
to use military force without hurting anyone, though the
purpose of military force is, or was up to recent years, to hurt

---

[1] This is where the Korean analogy would break down. In Korea it was *not*
militarily imperative to bomb the Chinese airfields and industries in Manchuria.
But if the U.N. forces had been faced with the prospect of surrendering *en masse* or
being driven into the sea by the Chinese armies are we sure that we should not
have used everything we had, including nuclear weapons, to stave off this disaster?
I do not see American troops being abandoned to their fate until *every* effort had
been made to save them.

the enemy as quickly and extensively as possible. Militarily the
operation was absurd and we either ought never to have started
it, or else swooped on Egypt within 12 hours and knocked the
hell out of her. Therefore it became a fiasco. We were defeated
by Colonel Nasser in the field of political warfare where he won
a series of tactical victories which caused our military defeat.[1]

At various periods during the slow build-up there were large
concentrations of British and French forces at sea. Supposing
the Russians had said to Nasser: "You have been bombed;
most foully and wantonly stabbed in the back. Three first-class
bombers are arriving to help you. Each carries a nuclear bomb.
Put an Egyptian pilot in each plane, the crew will be in plain
clothes. Send them out to drop one bomb on the naval trans-
ports at night and one on Malta. As soon as they have completed their mission the bombers will fly back to Russia. You
had better give Malta an hour's notice." Supposing Nasser
had replied: "Much obliged for your kind suggestion. I notice
that there is one spare bomb and I propose to send Paris an
ultimatum that unless a peace-plane arrives in Cairo with
accredited plenipotentiaries within 12 hours I shall drop a
nuclear bomb on a selected French target. For your private
information I think Lyons would be suitable, it is nicely
cupped in hills and the result will probably cause the Rhône to
be dammed and flood the valley up-stream. I shall report the
action to U.N. and have a clear case for acting in self-defence
in face of aggressive French and British military action."

Perhaps all this seems fantastic to you, but it only needed
two men, Khrushchev and Nasser, to make it not a speculation
but a new chapter in war.

VII

Although one of the difficulties inherent in the analysis of
the problems discussed in this chapter is that what shall be
considered as "major aggression" has not, and perhaps never
can be, defined or even described, there are certain forms of
aggression still possible which are clearly not major and belong
in a sense to the pre-nuclear age—at any rate for the time being.

[1] "What should we have done?" Briefly, the answer is that Britain should have
manoeuvred politically to become an U.N. police force separating the combatants
and occupying the Canal Zone with the backing of the Assembly.

I am referring to such episodes as the Mau Mau rebellion; or the possibility of an attack by the Yemenites on the Aden protectorate; or an Abyssinian aggression on British Somalis; or even the need to support the civil police in Britain in case of riots. I regard this type of aggression as being different in character from the kind of aggression we have in mind when we think of the Soviet Union.

They are usually robbery aggressions, without much ideological content. I do not rule out an element of robbery in a potential Russian aggression, but experience has shown that in disputes between major states it is exceedingly difficult, if not impossible, for the victor to indulge in large-scale robbery, or to use a more polite term, reparations, without doing himself a lot of damage. The more primitive the victor-state the more economically profitable it is to seize the economic assets of the vanquished.

As regards the lesser aggressions which require police action, it is my view that armed force has a part to play. Armed forced required for this purpose would clearly be relatively small and no question of using the H-bomb or any nuclear weapon would arise. The defence requirements for this type of police action should be the responsibility of an international body such as U.N., and I shall welcome a development in which U.N. will have its permanent police force, although there are obviously great difficulties in deciding under whose orders it should operate.

It is not my contention that one can be sure that the strategy of basing our defence on the existence of the H-bomb as a deterrent is bound to be ineffective; *it is my submission that its efficacy must be a matter of complete speculation with the grave disadvantage that if we have guessed wrong, the penalty of failure is the destruction of the nation.*

There are other aspects of the nuclear age which are far from being speculative. They are:

(*a*) The very grave danger that, unless the whole business of nuclear warfare is placed under firm international control at an early date, it is certain that the number of states owning nuclear weapons will increase. Already the British Minister of Defence in July 1957 stated in the House of Commons that the

Government regard it as unacceptable that Britain should be in an inferior position to the U.S.A. and the U.S.S.R. in the technique of manufacturing and producing stock-piles of nuclear weapons. The chances of effective international control seem to be poor. There is the further point that if tactical nuclear weapons are to become increasingly important in Nato they will have to be distributed amongst all the national contingents in Nato. The French (and British) have already used for non-Nato operations weapons supplied by the U.S.A. exclusively for use in Nato.

(*b*) Therefore the scene is set for a nuclear arms race and the development of the "clean" bomb makes the race seem more reasonable.

(*c*) Every arms race in the past designed to procure a balance of force has led to an explosion. What reasons have we for hoping that the nuclear arms race will be an exception to the rule? Especially now that tactical nuclear weapons are being looked upon as conventional! I doubt whether, if these nuclear weapons are developed and stock-piled, they will for ever remain in store.

(*d*) The political tensions which produce the armaments are still there and until they are reduced or eliminated there is the danger that they will degenerate into violence and within a few years "violence", i.e. military operations, will be conventionally conducted with nuclear weapons.

This last mentioned conclusion is the most sinister and alarming. Whatever may be our hopes and the prospects of a reduction of tension between the democratic and Communist camps, it is not likely to take place quickly because it will and can only be genuinely achieved through the acceptance by the majority of mankind of either the Communist or the free way of life.

All nations sufficiently powerful to jeopardize world peace must be in one camp before there can be peace. As long as there are two camps, in each of which the nations base their way of life on *one* of two philosophies, each of which is by its nature basically hostile to the other, there will be no peace, there *can* be no peace, but only an uneasy armistice.

Until the arrival of the nuclear age it was possible to assess the violence potential of a nation in terms of manpower and industrial strength. But if nuclear weapons become common-form and owned by all or nearly all the nations those criteria go by the board.

If we exclude the question of fall-out, which may be eliminated through using clean bombs, the nuclear weapon is simply an economical (in the military sense) method of obtaining a large explosion in concentrated form. One can suppose, for example, that the smallest tactical nuclear weapon is equivalent in destructive power to what could have been achieved in 1944 by 100 (or 1,000?) planes each dropping 2,000 lb. of bombs, or in 1918 by a concentration of 2,000 (or 20,000?) 6-in. Howitzers. The use of nuclear energy for military purposes has produced a situation in which IF *werre* (see page 22) or the conflict of ideas between sovereign states degenerates into violence (i.e. military operations) the violence is bound to be nuclear, and if it be nuclear it will be so violent that it ceases to be a means to an end and becomes an end in itself—the end being total destruction. It is hard to see how in the modern interdependent world any state in conflict of ideas with another state can be advantaged by the total destruction of its enemy. A possible exception—it could be argued—is to be found in the Israel-Arab dispute in which it must be assumed there are Arabs who wish to see the complete elimination of Israel, but this dispute has an exceptional background. Even in this case the Arab propaganda declares that it is the elimination of the state of Israel rather than Jews as such which is needed. Anti-Israel sentiments are not comparable to Nazi anti-semitism.

We must ask ourselves this question: "If the contribution of violence (i.e. military operations) to the settlement of differences of opinion or conflicts (*werre*) between sovereign states has evolved to such intensity that it is totally destructive, has not violence outlived its usefulness in disputes between large states?" It looks to me as if this is the truth. Bearing in mind that in major disputes violence has become equated with nuclear energy violence, I am forced to consider what possibilities are open to us if we exclude violence from our defence plans on the grounds that violence has become our master instead of our slave.

CHAPTER SEVEN

THE ROLE OF POLITICAL WARFARE

In Chapter V the possibilities and limitations of the use of military force in the task of defending our way of life were considered. In Chapter VI the degree to which the military force possessed by the United Kingdom and our allies was capable of fulfilling its function was examined. An account of the contribution political or psychological force can make to our defence arrangements must be added.

The use of political warfare operations in a struggle of ideas with another state falls into three categories when the struggle —as is the case in the war of ideas between Communism and democracy—is being waged on a stage of world dimensions.

There are the operations designed to strengthen psychologically our home front, those intended for uncommitted states and those designed to influence the enemy population.[1]

Before I consider these types of operation in further detail, mention must be made of one factor applicable to them all.

It cannot be too strongly stressed that all democratic political warfare operations must be inspired by democratic principles. This may strike the reader as an absurd platitude but experience in World Wars I and II showed that, if political warfare operations are (as they were) subservient to short term military requirements, the propaganda becomes confused, contradictory and liable to have a boomerang effect.[2]

That democratic political warfare must be sincerely conducted is the psychological equivalent of the fact that in the field of military operations democracies cannot launch preventive wars and remain democratic. This limitation of the offensive does not apply to the battle of the ideas because the

---

[1] Parallel activities drawn from military operations (say) in World War I would be: (a) Home propaganda and recruiting, (b) economic pressure on neutrals, (c) military operations overseas.

[2] Some interesting observations about political warfare are to be found in three lectures by Mr. Richard Crossman, M.P., published in the *R.U.S.I. Journal*, Nos. 587, 591, 592.

war is already in being. Even if our government had felt convinced in 1939 that Hitler intended to attack Poland and even knew of his decision to do so, it could not either legitimately or morally have launched a military attack on him as a preventive action. But to have waged intense political warfare from a much earlier date than 1939 against Hitler would have been perfectly in order. Furthermore we had not the means to wage a preventive military operation even had it been permissible; we had all that it required to wage political warfare, except the will to do it. The sudden guarantee to Poland was a very feeble psychological blow because it was not apparent to anyone how it was to be implemented, least of all to the British General Staff or to this author who was in Warsaw at the time and was obliged to depress Poles by assuring them that it was most unlikely the British Government intended to send "the great British Navy" into the Baltic. As a deterrent the British gesture was useless.

TRUTH must be the dominating feature of democratic propaganda. The truth, the whole truth and nothing but the truth. It may sometimes seem that to tell the truth is inconvenient and harmful to the cause, but in the long run it is the decisive weapon. It is not a secret weapon.

Democratic political warfare—unlike Communist operations —must be based on a wide foundation in the nation, and the object of the operation on the Home Front must be to ensure that the people understand the nature of the ideological struggle, the consequences of defeat, the values of our way of life and their supreme importance.

Another principle of importance is that democratic political warfare shall be inspired by a sense of mission. A nation which holds that the free way of life is the Truth must wish to see that way of life accepted universally. For democracy is not a static affair devoid of any mission. It is—so I believe—the right way of life and if a man believes this to be true it is his plain duty—quite apart from self-interest—to labour (by all methods compatible with democratic principles) to spread the gospel amongst peoples who for one reason or another are denied its benefits.

We are not entitled as democrats to give a negative answer to the question: Am I my brother's keeper?

The innumerable examples in history of occasions when the democratic peoples have sadly failed in their duty illustrate that the practice of democracy is hard and exacting. The acquiescence during the period 1935-39 by British public opinion and the British Government in the barbarous persecution in Germany by the Nazis of Jews and political opponents of the Nazi régime on the grounds (publicly stated by British Ministers) that it was no concern of ours what went on within the frontiers of Germany, was a grave error of policy as well as a moral lapse.

Whilst it is the duty (often unrealized or ignored) of democrats to promote their philosophy of life, we must understand that it is the duty (always realized and never ignored) of Communists to promote in every possible way their ideas about the right way of life. The Communist who, in contrast to the rather apathetic and static attitude of the democrat, adopts a dynamic approach to his task, has always realized that in a struggle which is essentially ideological the use of violence has its place but *not* the first place.

In a democracy such as Great Britain most people take our way of life for granted. They are so accustomed to its benefits that they regard them as being as certain as to-morrow's sunrise. One must recognize that many citizens would only begin to appreciate our way of life after they had lost it. Nevertheless the more thoughtful members of the community do understand that perpetual vigilance is the price of liberty and the activities of these people should be encouraged.

If we limit our definition of the phrase "the Home Front" to the United Kingdom, the less the Government concerns itself with direct propaganda the better.[1] The role of the Government should be to produce facts, to provide money for education and in general create a framework of law and order within which our way of life can lead a vigorous and intellectually expanding existence. The business of encouraging and assisting our people to feel that our way of life is something of importance to each individual, something which is as indispensible to him as he is to it, is the job of all the institutions which are the apparatus of our way of life. It is impossible in this book to go into details about ways and means of what can be broadly

[1] But see also Chapter XIV.

described as education for citizenship and all that need be
said is that those who for one reason or another have some
influence over the thoughts of their fellows—i.e., politicians,
journalists, teachers, broadcasters, Trade Union leaders,
managers, church leaders and elected leaders of all kinds—
have at this time a special responsibility and duty of an educational character. If however we extend the meaning of the
phrase "home front" to include the associations of democratic
nations, of which Nato is the most important example, then
governments should come more prominently into the picture,
partly because the task, or much of it, is beyond the technical
resources of private bodies, partly because the problem is that
of creating a common policy between sovereign states.

There is still a place for work by private bodies in this field
such as the Hansard Society for Parliamentary Government,
a supra-national body devoted to the cause of promoting the
institution of Parliamentary government.[1] The United Nations
Association is another example of the many unofficial organizations which exist to do educational work beyond the frontiers
of a single state about the free way of life or some aspect of it.
But where the governments should act and are the only bodies
which can act is in such matters as making a reality of Article II
of the Nato Treaty (see page 83). All the democratic nations
are agreed that their way of life is menaced by the Communist
political offensive and that however much (and rightly) their
ways of life differ in detail—and this is one of democracy's
glories—those ways of life are all based on certain principles
common to all. Yet, these nations have hardly begun to understand that if they are menaced by a monolithic Communist
doctrine, the democracies must be prepared to operate as a
democratic unit and apply democratic principles and practices
to their own international arrangements. This means a progressive abandonment of sovereignty and its absorption into a
higher loyalty. Because the true nature of war has been mis-
understood we have a considerable understanding of the need
for close co-operation amongst the democracies, *but only in the
military sphere*; and even here in 1957 there was still a nuclear
curtain between the U.S.A. and Great Britain.

Although the practical result in military co-operation

1 See Chapter XI, page 161.

between Nato powers falls short of what it could be, the idea is
there and the hideous word *Infrastructure* is evidence of it on
the ground; a common naval signal book illustrates it at sea,
and the English language is used in the air. The need to have
a good knowledge of English is one of the limiting factors in
recruiting pilots for the new German Air Force.

But politically the democratic world remains obstinately
"sovereign-state-minded" and this is a manifest and serious
weakness in the cold war with the Soviet Union. Without
attributing the blame to one side or the other it has been
unfortunate and harmful that, for the past decade, British and
American policy in the Middle East has so often been at cross-
purposes, culminating in the Suez quarrel at the very moment
when, owing to the Hungarian revolt, a united democratic
front was of great psychological importance.

The chief explanation of the striking difference between the
measure of unity in doctrine and practice which has been
achieved militarily between the Nato powers and the lack of
unity in the political field is to be found in the failure of the
Nato peoples and their leaders to understand that defence in
the present struggle embraces far more than military pre-
cautions.

Lord Ismay (then Secretary General of Nato) wrote in his
report on the first five years of Nato 1949-54: ". . . there is a
feeling in some quarters that member countries should examine
in Nato the methods of combating the massive anti-Nato
propaganda made by communists . . . a compromise has been
reached whereby Nato can act as a forum for consultation,
about psychological warfare. Such consultation is, however,
restricted to matters affecting member countries only: Nato, as
an international organization, has never envisaged carrying on
propaganda to the peoples of the Soviet Union or of the
satellite countries."[1]

The second category of political warfare operations is the
struggle for the allegiance of the uncommitted nations. Here
governments must play the major role although (especially
in all matters touching racial and colour questions) the individual who has the opportunity of behaving democratically
towards a citizen of one of these states can do a lot of good

[1] *Nato, The First Five Years 1949-54* by Lord Ismay, Chapter XIV, page 155.

especially as it must be conceded that the Soviet Union's policy is conspicuously non-racial. Similarly, one example of non-democratic behaviour can do immense damage.[1] A good example of constructive action against Communist propaganda and penetration has been the granting of self-government by Britain to Asian and African nations.

On the other hand the *Apartheid* policy in the Union of South Africa, which cannot possibly be regarded as democratic, is a very definite weakness in the political warfare armoury of the democracies especially if the latter take up the attitude that this is not their business. Economic activities by the democracies in the uncommitted nations *without political strings attached* are of great importance in the over-all political struggle and here again this weapon for combating Communist activities is much more potent if it is wielded in a collective manner by the democratic states.

Finally, there are the operations directed towards the "enemy" public opinion. In this case governmental action, especially when the enemy is a totalitarian state, is essential.

There is an extraordinary delusion prevalent in democratic countries that "public opinion" in totalitarian states is unimportant. On the contrary any dictator or oligarchy which knows its business regards the control of public opinion as a task of urgent and continuous priority. The totalitarian régime has a double problem. It must not only indoctrinate its own people with its ideology, but it must take measures to prevent its public hearing what the opponents of the régime have to say.

The domestic public opinion of a totalitarian régime is the Achilles' heel of the régime and the Soviet Union is no exception to this rule.

This therefore is the most important category of political warfare operations since a victory on this battlefield will "win the war" and could do so without a shot fired or a bomb dropped.

The truth of these observations is well illustrated if we examine what has happened in the Soviet Union. I will take youth as my example.

[1] e.g. The racial dispute at Little Rock, Arkansas in 1957 was world news and obscured all progress being made in integrating schools elsewhere in the South.

Speaking at the Third Congress of the Komsomol (Soviet Young Communist League) on 2nd October, 1920,[1] Lenin said: "The generation whose representatives are about 50 years old cannot expect to see the Communist society. This generation will die out before then. But the generation which is now 15 years old will see the Communist society, will itself build this society. And it must realize that the whole purpose of its life is to build this society." He pointed out, however, that this could be achieved only through the thorough indoctrination of youth with Communist ideology. "Only by radically remoulding the teaching, organization and training of youth shall we be able to ensure that the results of the efforts of the younger generation will be the creation of a society that will be unlike the old society, i.e. a Communist society." He maintained that the "whole object of training, educating and teaching the youth of to-day should be to imbue them with Communist ethics". Communist ethics and morality were then defined by Lenin as being entirely "derived from the interests of the class struggle of the proletariat". He linked the acquisition of knowledge with four concrete tasks: the defence of Communism, the interpretation of all knowledge from a Marxist viewpoint, the elimination of traces of other ideologies from the mind and the task of making the Soviet Union a mighty industrial country through collective effort.

On 13th April, 1928, Stalin made it clear that the next generation must be educated in such a way as would ensure the perpetual existence of a Communist government. A similar attitude exists in the satellite states. There is no space in which to describe how this indoctrination takes place in practice via the *Young Pioneers* (9-14 years), the *Komsomol* (14-26 years) and the continuation of indoctrination in the Trade Union organization, collective farms, university, etc., and via a host of other bodies. It begins even at the kindergarten stage. The reader who is interested can find ample and fully documented accounts of all this, providing irrefutable proof of the vital importance attached by the Communist leaders to "correct thinking" on the home front and this proof includes the text books which show that correct thinking emphasizes the "role of British and

[1] Lenin, *Works*, 4th Edition, Vol. 31, pp. 258-75   State Publishing House of Political Literature, Moscow, 1950.

American Imperialism in the war against the forces of peace and democracy"[1] (i.e. the Communist states).

What is of current importance in the Soviet Union and has a direct bearing on the aspect of defence under review in this Chapter is the revolt of Communist youth (and the intellectuals) which has become significant since the upheaval caused by the denunciation of Stalin. By the middle of 1957 there had been authentic news of student unrest in 10 Soviet Union republics. There had been rioting in Georgia, barracking at official lectures, boycotting of indoctrination classes; dissemination of news from outside sources, illegal publications, refusal to volunteer for work in backward areas and so forth.

It would take us too far afield to pursue this subject in detail, but there is plenty of evidence that at no time during the past decade have the possibilities for a constructive political warfare attack on the minds of the young people beyond the Iron Curtain been more hopeful than at this moment (1957).

The denunciation of Stalin and Stalinism set in train a series of events which, from the defence point of view in the field of psychological warfare, are full of promise. All over the Communist world, in the Soviet Union, in Poland, Hungary and the other satellites, in China and in Northern Vietnam and even in Yugo-Slavia, two phenomena or trends had become clear by 1957. First, during the period of relaxation which succeeded the exposure of Stalinism, the intellectuals bubbled up in a ferment of long-suppressed freedom. Startling books began to appear, reflecting the kind of idea which caused so notable a figure as Professor Kantorowitz to confess with bitterness after he had fled from East Germany:

"I can no longer refuse to recognize the tragic paradox . . . that I myself have contributed my mite in helping to bring about the very thing that I meant to fight against; the very lawlessness, the exploitation of the workers, the spiritual enslavement of the intelligentsia, the arbitrary rule of an unworthy clique. . . . Fascism and barbarism had again risen behind our backs—in word, thought and deed in the offices of the Party bureaucracy."

The second phenomenon was the inevitable reaction by the

[1] From the *Programme for Teaching the English Language*.

bosses to this revolt which, in one way or another, was being suppressed towards the end of 1957; suppressed but not destroyed and the counter-revolution beyond the Iron Curtain will rise again. Too many people have had a glimpse of what life could be and it looked good, so they will return to the attack.

Another important feature of this third category of political warfare is that an attack on the minds of the "enemy" population fulfils the requirements of the principle that the best method of defence is to attack.

By a vigorous and sustained psychological offensive against the enemy he can be thrown on to the defensive and obliged to impose restriction on his people, such as jamming of broadcasts, which may cause his public to have subversive thoughts and ask awkward questions.

It is part of our creed or faith that all men are liberty and freedom loving and that if the people of a great nation, be they Germans or Russians, are supporting ideas and practices which are undemocratic it must be due to a lack of knowledge and understanding of the truth on their part and it is both our duty and to our self-interest to endeavour to let them know the truth.

In this chapter I have outlined some theoretical considerations about the role of political warfare operations in the defence of our way of life against political attack. In Chapter VIII some suggestions will be made as to how these principles could be better translated into practice than they are at present, with a consequent strengthening of our defences in the struggle of ideas with the Soviet Union.

CHAPTER EIGHT

OUR POLITICAL DEFENCE

PRECEDING CHAPTERS have been concerned with the nature of the attack on our way of life (the defence of which I have postulated is the prime purpose of our defence arrangements); the role of military force in this task and the capacity of our military force to achieve it; and the part political warfare can play in defence. To complete the picture, our political warfare arrangements must be surveyed in relation to their capacity to fulfil their role.

At the present time (1957) it is recognized that some psychological activity on our part is called for in response to the massive psychological offensive ceaselessly operated by the Communists. But political warfare is not regarded at the highest level as an integral part of defence. The nearest we come to this recognition is a reference in some of the White Papers on defence to "Communist penetration and infiltration" but a careful search of these annual pronouncements fails to reveal any proposals for political warfare. They are all documents dealing with the armed forces and the only reference which seems to connect up with political warfare is a passage in the 1956 statement which reads (in part) ". . . by the goodwill that it engenders in foreign countries, the Navy is a valuable weapon in the cold war against Communism" (para 21).

An outline of the use which has been made of political warfare during the past fifty years is as follows. It provides us with a background to the present situation:

In World Wars I and II (which according to my opinion began about 1906 and 1933 respectively) practically no place was assigned to political warfare in our defence arrangements until the wars degenerated in 1914 and 1939 into military operations.

In World War I it was not until 20th February, 1917 that the Department of Information was created, to be superseded by a Ministry of Information on 4th March, 1918 which included, under Lord Northcliffe, a directorate of propaganda in enemy countries. Dr. Mitchell who worked in this organization has written that:

"The inspiring principle of the new organization was that propaganda should depend upon policy."

But he adds:

"If a concerted policy did exist, it was unknown to those who were conducting propaganda. The wiser propagandists . . . endeavoured to limit themselves to a restricted field from which declared 'war aims' and ultimate terms of peace were excluded."[1]

In 1933 Josef Goebbels was created Reich Minister of Propaganda and Public Enlightenment, and as the German Press, radio and all instruments for disseminating information were under his control and he had immense funds at his disposal in addition to the sanction of the concentration camp, he achieved a considerable success in his task of indoctrinating a nation with Hitler's ideas.

It has seemed to me most extraordinary that the British Government took no steps to counter the Nazi propaganda —or for that matter to deal earlier with that of Mussolini. It was late in the day for the British Prime Minister to tell the German people on 3rd September, 1939 we were not fighting them but were fighting to free them, when for five or six years we had accepted without protest Dachau and Nazi bestialities or, at the best, emulated the priest who "passed by on the other side".

It was a good thing that some British Members of Parliament visited Belsen in 1946; it would have been better if some M.P.'s had tried to visit Dachau in 1936.

In the twelve months preceding military operations in World War II some steps were taken to prepare the outline of an embryonic Ministry of Information. I know something about this from the inside and of the pitiful and inadequate plans that were made. At one time the director-general designate was a civil servant and half an hour's conversation

[1] *Encyclopaedia Britannica*, Vol. 32, page 181.

with this gentleman was enough to convince me that unconsciously he was one of Hitler's secret weapons!

When military operations began, the Ministry of Information sprang into life and, under a procession of Ministers, became both the home of advertising agency personnel and something approaching a public scandal until the Rt. Hon. Brendan Bracken, M.P. took charge.

Before the war a Political Warfare Executive (P.W.E.) was established. It was a secret department in the Foreign Office. It was also linked to the Chiefs of Staff Committee. In matters of foreign policy it was responsible to the Foreign Secretary but, in the words of Mr. Crossman, M.P., who was a senior officer in the organization, "for all strategic matters there was also continuous control by the Chiefs of Staff to ensure that our propaganda conformed to their strategic requirements". P.W.E. became a very large organization and was responsible for propaganda in leaflet and radio form, both "white" and "black"[1] propaganda. In 1941 the activities of P.W.E. were integrated with those of the two American organizations, the Office of Strategic Services (O.S.S.) and the Office of War Information (O.W.I.). The first was secret, the second public— very public. At the end of the war the main impetus of our propaganda was coming from an Anglo-American staff under the Supreme Commander at Shaef.

A survey of what was done up to the end of World War II leads to the conclusion that political warfare, both in its black and white manifestations, was simply regarded as an activity which, in many different ways, could be of assistance to the military conduct of the war. And it was so regarded by those who worked in this branch of defence. Nothing could be more revealing than a remark of Mr. Crossman's, when he said: *"Psychological warfare is not a substitute for action* . . . it is at best an accompaniment to action, something which slightly accelerates the process of military force. . . ."

The generally accepted and official view of the role of political warfare and the limits which have been assigned to it could not have been stated more concisely. Yet what an absurd

---

[1] *White* propaganda was official and what it purported to be, the voice of the Allies;
Black propaganda purported to come from inside the enemy country.

statement it is if we remember the simple and irrefutable fact that an IDEA *must* precede action!

Should you see fit to purchase a copy of this book your *action* will be agreeable to author, publisher and bookseller, but none of us are expecting to sell many copies to persons who, with a vacant look on their faces, buy the book without having some thought in their minds related to the subsequent act of purchase.

It is my conviction that, had the true nature of war been understood in the period between the wars, and had proper use been made of all the potentialities of political warfare against dictatorships, World War II could have been won before it degenerated into military action in 1939. Leaving that aside, a proper understanding of the power of political warfare could have greatly shortened the length of the second World War. The greatest psychological stroke in World War II carried out by the Allies was the announcement of unconditional surrender, and it was a stab in their own backs! In April 1944 General Eisenhower, on the advice of his psychological warfare staff, sent a paper to President Roosevelt which said in effect: "We accept the policy of unconditional surrender, but we would like to be able to tell a German General in Normandy how he should surrender if he wants to." A reply came back via Mr. Stettinius that politics were to be left to the politicians!

Though it was a tragedy that political warfare was so neglected from 1914-45, it can at least be said that military operations still had some logic in them and had not become so destructive as to be absurd. But the nuclear age has completely altered the traditional relationship between military and political warfare operations. The subservience of political warfare to military consideration was foolish in 1914, absurd in 1939 and is madness in 1957.

We come now to World War III which began in 1946. During the past decade some progress in the recognition of the importance of political warfare has been made. This is due—I suggest—not so much to inner conviction on the part of democratic governments, but simply because ever since the Communists have been in power, but especially since 1946, they have been so active on the political warfare front that their efforts called forth some reaction in kind from their prospective

victims. But the effort from our side has been meagre; co-
operation with our allies is loose and the sums spent are
derisory. When in 1957 it became evident that the British
position in the Middle East had been successfully dealt a series
of body blows by political warfare operations ex-Cairo, of
which a typical example was the expulsion of Glubb Pasha from
Jordan, the Government decided to step up our political warfare in the Middle East, but in announcing extra expenditure
on these services they also made economies in existing services
to other parts of the world.

*   *   *

Some years after the end of World War II, I sought an
interview with the Minister of Defence and asked whether he
agreed that political warfare was part of our defence arrang-
ments. He did. I then suggested that if we included in the
expenditure on political warfare, every activity, public, secret,
official and private designed to promote knowledge of and
belief in our way of life in contra-distinction to the Communist
doctrine, the total annual expenditure might be in the region of
£10 million or about 1 per cent of the expenditure on our
armed forces at that time. He thought this to be a reasonable
estimate. I then asked him whether as Minister of Defence he
had any Cabinet responsibility for the allocation of this trivial
sum. He said: "No." Finally I suggested that he might consider
setting up an inter-departmental committee charged with the
task of reporting upon the relationship between political warfare and military operations (including preparations for the
use of force) in the over-all strategy of Total War, and that I
hoped such a Committee would recommend the creation of the
post of a fourth member of the Chiefs of Staff Committee, a
person to be called the C.P.W. (Chief of Staff Political Warfare).

The Minister seemed quite interested but . . . the rest of the
talk must unfortunately remain off the record.

*   *   *

It is not possible for an unofficial person to obtain a complete
account of the whole set-up of our political warfare arrangements at this time (1957) and there are no doubt aspects of it
which it would be tactically unwise to discuss in public. But

enough is public property to make it safe to assert that it is all pretty small beer. During the past five years the Americans have attached more importance to this aspect of the Cold War than the British and they have spent (and misspent) a good deal of money on it through official and unofficial channels. Radio Free Europe at Munich is a large semi-official American organization in parallel with the official Voice of America. My impression is that the Americans are less competent operators than the British but that the latter have to function on a shoe string. There is some collaboration between the British and Americans and possibly between Nato powers in general, but in a small way and it is difficult to get details. This collaboration takes place at Under-Secretaries level. In Britain the Foreign Office is the Ministry chiefly responsible for psychological warfare and a junior Minister is in charge.

Another impression I have is that in the whole defence picture, the organizations official, semi-official and unofficial which are engaged in psychological or political warfare against the Soviet Union can be fairly compared to the role played by the army bands and Kneller Hall in the fighting capacity of the British Army. A worthy side line.

What is required without delay is a White Paper on Defence incorporating political warfare and military warfare arrangements in one comprehensive picture. If this is asking for too big a cherry at one mouthful, then may we not have a Political Warfare White Paper? The trouble about this would be that its author would have to ask our Cabinet and other Governments what the policy was, and we have seen in our studies of military white papers how difficult it has been for our Government to make up its mind about policy in military defence.

The policy statement in a Political Warfare White Paper should be much easier to produce, but only if the Cabinet is in a frame of mind which appreciates the true nature of war, and the importance of the battle of ideas, and if there existed a common U.S.A.-U.K. political policy in defence of democracy. Of this there are no signs but plenty of evidence to the contrary.

*   *   *

I will conclude this chapter by giving some illustrations of proposals for political warfare operations which occurred to me at various times and which were submitted to the appropriate authorities. It is not claimed that they were very wonderful and their father puts them forward with diffidence, but they do illustrate the kind of operation I regard as worth considering in political warfare.

Case I. *Object: The overthrow of Mussolini.*

Time approximately 1934-35. About this time Mussolini was making violent speeches against the democracies and referring to them as dung-heaps. It was proposed that certain discreditable financial transactions in which leading Fascists were involved should be ferreted out by appropriate agencies and, when all the facts were clearly proved, the whole business exposed in a printed document to be posted up in large letters in our Embassy grounds and all consulates-general offices in Italy entitled "News from Italy". The document would also have been circulated all over the world and broadcast to Italy. "The Duce says we are a dung-heap but listen to this. . . ." I anticipated considerable reactions in the industrial areas of Northern Italy. My argument was that since the Italian people had been told by their leader that we were dung-heaps and that Italy must "live dangerously" there was no reason against, and many for, the idea that we should do our best to open the eyes of the Italians to the nature of the cess-pit of Fascism and what "living dangerously"[1] would lead to.

Case II. *Object: To deal with Hitler's demands on Czechoslovakia in 1938.*

It was suggested that:[2] Czechoslovakia be recommended not to resist German demands by force of arms, but to adopt so far as possible a non-co-operative and passive resistance attitude, as was done by Germans in the Ruhr in 1923. That Great Britain, France and Russia and as many other states as can be persuaded to do so, inform Germany that, although in order to avoid bloodshed, Czechoslovakia has been advised to submit for *the time being* to superior force, Germany will be considered an

[1] Mussolini's slogan for the Italian people.
[2] Full details are to be found in *News-Letter* 115 of 16th September, 1938.

outlaw state until such time as she abandons her claims on Czechoslovakia and behaves as a civilized state. Concurrently with this announcement it was proposed that Great Britain and France be placed on a war footing. In the U.K. call up reserves. Put A.R.P. into full operation. Rehearse evacuation of cities. Mobilize industry for war. Begin food control. Establish a register of National Service. Limit profits. Broaden the base of Government by the inclusion of Liberal and Socialist ministers. Withdraw diplomats and all British nationals from Germany. Expel all German nationals (other than Jews and refugees) from British and French territories. Break off all commercial intercourse with Germany and restrict trade with neutrals as required to prevent leaks. Forbid access of German shipping to British and French ports. Broadcast continuously to the German people explaining that there is no hostility towards them but only to Hitler and the Nazi régime. Inform Germany that any military action taken by her in consequence of this non-intercourse policy will meet with armed retaliation.

This was an outline of a strategy compounded of psychological war and economic pressure which I recommended should be adopted in preference to starting World War II by military operations (for which we were not prepared) for the rescue of Czechoslovakia. I have been told the full document was considered by a Cabinet sub-committee and, writing nearly twenty years after those tragic and fatal days which culminated in the Munich settlement, I believe the proposals were sound. If violent military operations are considered to be the *only* way to change the enemy's mind, then, in terms of the military forces at our disposal in 1938, "Munich" was the only military answer.

But the "White War" as I called my plan, was another answer which made sense, provided the meaning and object of war are understood. I claimed that some of the advantages of the White War would have been: (*a*) The onus of retaliating by an armed attack against non-intercourse would have rested on the Nazis and we ought to have been able to ensure that this caused them trouble with the German people. It is difficult to justify an assault on a man because he will not admit you to his society. (*b*) By adopting this plan we should have avoided the dreadful danger that, in all the confusions and uncertain

developments of a rapidly-launched world war, the fundamental issue of "democracies" versus "totalitarian states"
would be obscured, and: (c) Before this issue was decided on
the battlefields it was advisable to ensure a preliminary period
in which the democracies could organize a world on their own,
isolated in every respect from the totalitarian world. Some of
these 1938 ideas (quite apart from the nuclear problem) have
relevance in 1957.

Case III. *Object: To separate the Nazis from the German people.*
    In the summer of 1939, having visited Warsaw and Berlin, I
returned to London convinced that, late though the hour was,
an effort must be made to open the eyes of the German people
to the perils towards which they were allowing Hitler to lead
them and mankind. Since Government would take no action,
private enterprise attempted this great task. A series of special
news-letters in German were sent to thousands of Germans. It
is impossible in these pages to spare the space to describe the
operational details, but the results exceeded our most optimistic
hopes. It was, of course, much too little too late and was no
more than a pilot scheme. But it seriously disturbed the Nazi
leaders, who mobilized all their resources against this private
psychological warfare operation. It caused our Ambassador
in Berlin to press our Government to try to stop this activity
because it was greatly upsetting Hitler and Goebbels, who were
convinced it was sponsored by the British Government. It had
many other results, too numerous to specify here, some of
which were only revealed after 1945. Amongst the results was
the fact that the last paragraph of the last official communication Hitler sent to H.M.G. was solely concerned with abuse of
the present writer. I often wonder what might have been
achieved with £5,000,000 from 1936 to 1939 when I examine
what was done with £5,000 in the last three months of so-called
peace.[1]

Case IV. *Object: To expose the hypocrisy of Peaceful Co-existence.*
    The Bulganin-Khrushchev visit in 1956. The proposal was
that the Prime Minister should invite the two Russian leaders

[1] Full details of this operation and the texts of the letters are in *Total Victory*
by S. King-Hall (Faber and Faber).

to appear with him on television and say in effect (after giving
due notice) "we are all peace lovers and we ought to get to
know each other better. I have a proposal to make which I hope
will meet with your agreement. I suggest that 100,000 young
Russians should come over at our expense and live for a fort-
night in English homes. I daresay there are 15,000,000 people
looking at this programme and, if you will agree in principle
to accept our invitation, I will ask any of these people now
looking and listening to us to write at once to the B.B.C. if
they are willing to accommodate one or more young Russians.
We shall certainly receive thousands of letters. Will you please
comment on this?"

B. & K. would not have agreed to this proposal, in which
case their refusal should have been given maximum publicity,
especially in Russia. "Your leaders will not let you come and
see us! Why? Ask your leaders! We are peace loving, we wish
to know you better. Please press your leaders to let you come.
We may have much to learn from you."

*   *   *

There are numerous tactical operations of political warfare
which could be investigated and carried out at small expense,
if once the principle were accepted that political warfare
activities are extremely important, perhaps the most important,
part of our defence arrangements, and in charge of a Minister
of Cabinet rank with a political warfare Chief of Staff in the
C.O.S.'s committee. It can be said that the Secretary of State
for Foreign Affairs is the Cabinet Minister. My reply is that in
the Foreign Office political warfare is a subsidiary activity and
I suspect that it occupies the same menial relationship to
foreign policy as it did to military operations from 1940-45.
Heresy though it is, I want foreign policy to be the servant of
political warfare, or if you prefer it that foreign policy should
be political warfare.

E

PART TWO

INTRODUCTION TO PART TWO

I SUGGESTED ON page 13, that we must make a great effort to break through the thought-barrier which up till now has limited our mental activities about defence. In the first part of this book, which contains the homework which has to be done in preparation for the break through this barrier, we have reached a speed of Mach one. Now we must no longer be content with these experimental and reconnoitring flights but go all out to burst through the barrier and see what we find on the other side.

But first a brief summary of what has been written in Part One. The nature of war is a clash of ideas between sovereign states, from which it follows that the object of defence is the protection of our ideas against enemy ideas and the inculcation of our ideas into his mind. Our ideas are expressed in our way of life which is composed of principles and institutions. The nature of the attack at this time on our way of life is ideological, backed by force. The role of armed force in the general plan of defence is inappropriate against Soviet political attack, but can be useful to protect our institution against military attack. The extent to which our existing armed force fulfils its functions depends upon the efficiency of the great deterrent. Political warfare in the defence of our way of life must be based on TRUTH and have a sense of mission. Political warfare could be our most effective weapon but has played a secondary role to military force.

In the second part of this book I shall build up a new theory and practice of defence from the conclusions which emerge from Part One.

This is necessary because the broad conclusion which emerges from the factual investigation in Part One of our defence arrangements is that they suffer from some disadvantages, certainly very serious, possibly fatal.

Statements made in the autumn of 1957 by the British Minister of Defence revealed that we were then in a position in which the main role of our defence forces *was to protect themselves* against a nuclear attack, so that even if the unprotected nation were destroyed the armed forces would survive and be capable of dealing the retaliatory blow. This is almost as if in World War I naval strategists had been reduced (in 1917) to saying: "We cannot protect the U.K. against the U-boats and we must anticipate that the U-boat blockade will bring the nation to its knees. But be comforted by the thought that the Royal Navy has been withdrawn from the U.K. to bases elsewhere in order to ensure that the blockade of the Central Powers will finally be decisive."

But the parallel is not exact, for in the nuclear age one must substitute the words "*the nation will be destroyed*" for the words "bring the nation to its knees". In 1957 we are saying: "We cannot prevent the house being burnt down but we can assure you the enemy pig will be roasted."

CHAPTER NINE

FINDING A NEW IDEA

THE NOTION THAT what we are striving to defend is
our way of life would perhaps be accepted by most thoughtful
people as a rather academic and theoretically correct statement
remote from the practical problems of defence. The same people
might agree that my outline of what we mean by our way of life
passes muster though it has been done more intelligently by
better equipped writers. I agree with that. They might also go
a long way with me in my submission that at this time the
attack on our way of life has a very large ideological content in
it, but I think they would say that the nub of the matter is to be
found in the defence of our homeland and those of our allies
and that, although it is true that nations can be conquered
from within, before we spend time thinking about abstract
matters such as the defence of the ideology of our way of life,
the first business on the agenda is to make sure that our enemies
do not occupy our territories, and that to prevent this occupation is the prime duty of our armed forces. I argued in Chapter
V that it is the function of our armed forces to defend our
institutions and this is what they have always succeeded in
doing up till now.

I was brought up to believe that in the words of the preamble
to the Articles of War: "On the British Navy, under the good
providence of God, the wealth, safety and strength of the kingdom chiefly depend." This was as true in 1914 as it had been
for centuries. Within my lifetime it has become a legend and
Rule Britannia is now a folk song. When the newly joined cadets
reached Osborne Naval College in 1906 they were fallen in
opposite a gallery under which the innocent eyes of these little
boys read a sentence set forth in polished brass letters a foot
high. It said:

THERE IS NOTHING THE NAVY CANNOT DO.

One small creature shocked his neighbour by whispering "Do you think that's true?" We were both to live to see it become a considerable over-statement.

To-day we must face some new facts. If we assume that when the democratic powers talk about "a major aggression" they mean a movement by Russian armed forces into a democratic state (and I do not find any evidence that the democracies are thinking about major political warfare aggression), then it is a *fact* that our principal defence against such an aggression is NOT the use of a weapon immediately the aggression starts or is threatened, but the assertion that, if the aggression includes nuclear war on the grand scale, we shall retaliate.[1] We have the H-bomb but everything indicates that it is not our policy to use it until it has been used to inflict unimaginable destruction upon us. No other policy is compatible with democratic principles. Were this not so it would have been plain common sense to have said to Stalin after the first Russian atomic explosion: "Unless you immediately cease working on nuclear weapons we will launch a nuclear war on you and *one more test* explosion from your side will unleash our stock-pile of atomic weapons on Russia since we, the democracies, are determined to retain a world monopoly of this decisive weapon."

It is arguable that it would have been proper to have taken up the attitude that God or Destiny, having enabled one nation (the U.S.A.) to acquire this weapon, the U.S.A., in order to atone for using it on Japan and thus inaugurating nuclear war, should have decided voluntarily to declare that it would place the nuclear weapon in the keeping of the U.N.[2] *However, all such notions are might-have-beens and the present situation is that our defence is founded on an* IDEA; *that of the deterrent of retaliation.*

II

If the reader is *not* to stay on the orthodox side of the thought barrier he should realize that our defence arrangements are now based almost entirely on an IDEA. The idea of the deterrent,

[1] This is putting it mildly. Some would argue that we have implied that a "major aggression" (whatever that is) will evoke a nuclear attack on the Soviet Union.
[2] The U.S. proposals in 1946 were somewhat in this sense (the Baruch proposals).

an idea linked to the physical existence of H-bombs, and the suicidal consequences of a major nuclear war.

There has always been a certain deterrent content in defence thinking and in defence arrangements. In the eleventh century a Saxon chronicler wrote that the Danes: "durst not maintain a fight with King William" who had built up a Navy after the humiliation of having had to emulate Ethelred and bribe a fleet of Northmen not to harry the East coast. There is a deterrent conception in the classical balance of power theory, but the H-bomb deterrent idea has some novel features as we have noted in Chapter VI. One can make a mental picture of the difference between a deterrent idea linked to doing something which may lead to a serious illness and one linked to action certain to lead to death.

The notion that our defence arrangements should be based on an idea, on the creation of a certain climate of thought in men's minds, both on our side and on that of the enemy is perfectly sound, but whether the present idea (which is certainly not the only one available) is the best is something which needs investigating. Each person must make up his own mind about this matter. So far as I am concerned the disadvantages of the nuclear deterrent seem so grave that I have reached the conclusion that there is a *prima facie* case for abandoning this foundation of our defence. In so grave a matter which involves a decision of world wide significance and the adoption of a policy which would be a reversal of all the defence thinking of the past, it would be arrogant for any individual to say: "I know." This is why I plead that the best minds in the country should be brought together to consider this question.

III

I start with the assumption that it is desirable to base the defence of our way of life on an IDEA as is the case at present, but that the H-bomb deterrent idea should be replaced by a better one. Where should we seek this idea? In the military or the political sphere?

The attack on our way of life is being carried out with a spear of which the blade or head is concerned with political attack and the shaft is military force. Another analogy would be a radio-set on a tank. The radio-set can start operating on the minds of the opponents long before the tank can crush their bodies.

Since it has been suggested that the Communist political attack is the most dangerous aspect of the assault on our way of life, it might seem that in trying to bring our defences up to date we ought to start with proposals for improving our political warfare arrangements but I have come to the conclusion that it will be best to defer this investigation until we have dealt with the military side *because this is where the H-bomb deterrent and all its disadvantages are located,* and if and when we can see how to replace that idea with a better one we shall be in a position to deal with the political side of defence.

The simplest way of considering the complex problem is to make the assumption that the British Government has unilaterally decided not to make, stock or use H-bombs.

We must examine what would be some of the consequences of this decision. An obvious result would be an economy amounting to many millions of pounds a year, but I regard this as only a desirable by-product. Much more important is that it is unlikely that the U.S.A. would follow our example. If the U.K. decided to contract out of the H-bomb business, the feeling in America might be something like this: "The British are sheltering under our decision to maintain H-bombs. This is the beginning of the end. If the British will not defend themselves to the limit of their capacities we had better write them off and retire into fortress America."

Similarly public opinion in Britain, if it refused to have anything to do with H-bombs would feel—at least I hope they would—that we could not take up the attitude that we relied for our defence on American H-bombs.

If we contracted out of the H-bomb business we must contract out of all connections which are associated with H-bombs and this means saying to the Americans: "Unless *you* abandon the H-bomb business the Anglo-American Alliance in its military aspects is at an end."

For example, if we unilaterally abandoned the H-bomb it would obviously be absurd to allow American planes with H-bombs to operate from British territory. If we abandoned the H-bomb I shall show in due course that tactical nuclear weapons would also have to be abandoned. This done we should be in the same non-nuclear weapon position as the Continental members of Nato and could maintain a military alliance with them on a non-nuclear basis.

The situation which would then arise would be as follows: Two great Powers, the U.S.A. and Russia, would be armed with nuclear weapons; Great Britain and the Continental powers would not have nuclear weapons. Canada would probably go along with the U.S.A.

It is a waste of time thinking in isolation of H-bombs, or clean bombs, or tactical nuclear weapons of 5, 10, 25 kilotons which then start becoming strategical weapons up to 25 megatons. The distinction to be made is between THE USE OF NUCLEAR ENERGY FOR EXPLOSIVE PURPOSES IN WAR AND ITS NON-USE. This is the idea we must examine. This idea is clear cut and precise. It is even more so than would have been the case if a decision had been called for in the Middle Ages as between war with gunpowder or without it.

If Great Britain decided as a deliberate act of policy to forswear the use of nuclear energy in war, Nato as it is at present would collapse and we should be left with the responsibility of creating E.T.O. (the European Treaty Organization). Politically it would mean that the European states would be endeavouring to contract out of a nuclear war between the two nuclear using states.

We must recognize that the chances are that war between Russia and the U.S.A. would be nuclear, or become so. It does not follow that the non-nuclear states would be successful in their attempts to keep out of the holocaust but they might have some hope of doing so.

A moral question arises here. We must assume that in any war between Russia and the U.S.A. the latter would be fighting for the right ideas. Are we entitled to be neutral in such a struggle or do we betray our own way of life if we adopt such an attitude?

This raises the whole issue of whether it is either morally right (the Pacifists have their answer to this one) or expedient to use violence in support of one's ideals, if the violence involved is so enormous that it causes such vast destruction that what we are trying to defend will be destroyed. My opinion is that the

invention of H-bombs and guided missiles has made it wrong
and inexpedient to use or prepare to use this extreme violence.
Some people will reply that catastrophic destruction and
enormous numbers of deaths, is better than slavery. This begs
the question. It assumes that if we contract out of the use of
such extreme violence and admit in advance that this is our
intention and in consequence are obliged to submit to Soviet
demands (which might include an occupation of our country)
all is lost. Is it? Is our way of life then killed for all time? I
shall return to this question in a moment.

Strenuous attempts are being made at this time (1957) to
limit or control in some way the use of large scale nuclear
weapons. I believe that for many reasons they will fail; one of
the chief reasons being the existence of the tactical nuclear
weapon.

If a conflict started between the Soviet Union and the West,
the Soviet Union might say: "We do not intend to use nuclear
weapons of any kind unless they are used on us." It would be to
their advantage to say this because they would have a superiority in non-nuclear force, and the Nato powers would be in an
awkward position. Are we to suppose that they would reply:
"We intend to use nuclear tactical weapons in order to counter-
balance your superiority in non-nuclear forces?" This would
mean that the West was deliberately making the war a nuclear
event and this would have serious disadvantages from the
western point of view. First, it would put the West in the wrong
with uncommitted world opinion; secondly, it would lead to a
split of opinions in the western countries; thirdly, it would open
the United Kingdom to nuclear attack and this is a form of
attack against which we are defenceless.

My surmise is that if the Soviet Union were clever enough to
make a statement about not using nuclear weapons and live up
to it we should have to follow suit, even though to-day we claim
that *we must and will use* tactical nuclear weapons in a Nato war.

If we decided not to use tactical nuclear weapons this would
mean (at least in the opening stages) a non-nuclear war and,
as the forces are deployed at this time (1957), it is difficult to
see how the Russians could be prevented from overrunning
Europe and launching a massive conventional attack with
airborne divisions on the United Kingdom, preceded and

accompanied by massive bombing and guided missile attacks across the Channel with non-nuclear weapons. Faced with imminent invasion, or perhaps with an invasion on the way to being successful, would the British Government decide that as our national existence appeared to be at stake we must abrogate our pledge not to use nuclear weapons (unless they are used by the enemy) by calling on the Americans to launch a nuclear attack on Russia? It is an open question whether we could rely on the Americans to make the war nuclear to save us from an occupation and whether it would be in our best interests to ask them to do so, and I am more sure that the British Government would think twice before taking such a step. My vote would be against it because I am convinced that as between Britain occupied by the Russian army and a Britain a smoking radioactive charnel-house the former is the lesser of two great evils.

In a major war in which for one reason or another nuclear weapons are not used (just as gas and bacteriological weapons were not used in World War II, and I have always believed that the bombing of cities was not initially the policy of either belligerent), the people of the U.K. must recognize that they are liable to invasion to a greater extent than ever before in their history. This is a strange idea to most Englishmen but the notion that one's country is liable to be invaded is familiar to Continental Europeans, Middle Easterners, Africans and Asians. We are unique amongst nations, not in the Western hemisphere, in not reckoning invasion of our homeland as one of the normal hazards of international life. We are no longer amongst the privileged class in this respect and should face this fact and take it into account in our defence plans.

In considering what modifications would be desirable in the military defence arrangements we maintain for the defence of our way of life against military attack, we started with the assumption that we ought to consider abandoning the H-bomb. This policy would inevitably and logically lead to a decision to eschew the use of nuclear energy for military purposes. I believe a number of people would be prepared to take the first step (i.e. abandon the H-bomb). For example the Bishop of Manchester said on 1st June, 1957: "(it is argued that) Russia's conventional arms can overrun us. We must possess some ultimate sanction. But do we intend to use it (the H-bomb)?

Ought we in any conceivable circumstances to use it? My answer is an unhesitating 'No'. It would be better to be defeated than to engage in H-bomb warfare. For when the last bomb has exploded you have lost what you were fighting for . . . there are risks no matter which way we turn, but is it not better to take a risk which is creative and can lead to no worse than material defeat, than to take one which may lead us into a defeat which has as its only compensation the total destruction of the enemy as well as ourselves . . . for realistic as well as spiritual reasons I believe that the best and wisest course would be unilaterally to renounce the use of the H-bomb."

Senator Morse of the U.S.A. said in the Senate on 23rd March, 1957: "I cannot bring myself to give continued support in the name of defence to a hydrogen bomb policy. . . ."

Concentration of thought on the horrors of the H-bomb has diverted attention from the tactical nuclear weapon which, like the housemaid's baby, may be only a little one, but if ever used will soon lead to the appearance of Big Brother H-bomb. Whether or not the many eminent persons who are prepared to consider abandoning the H-bomb, or who advocate its abandonment, realize that they must also support the abandonment of nuclear energy for military purposes, is unknown to me.

Those who advocate the abandonment of the H-bomb may not appreciate that by a kind of chain reaction in reverse, this decision also means a decision not only to abandon the use of nuclear energy in war but THE ABANDONMENT OF THE MAINTENANCE OF CONVENTIONAL WEAPONS FOR USE IN MAJOR WARS.

The reasons are as follows:

(a) If in a major war the Soviet Union decided to use nuclear weapons, they are so overwhelmingly more effective than conventional weapons that to invite conventional forces to fight forces armed with nuclear weapons is an absurdity.

(b) If we assume that the U.K. and the western European powers have abandoned nuclear weapons and that the Soviet Union, either for political reasons or because they do not wish to fight a nuclear war with the U.S.A., also decide not to use nuclear weapons, then the conventional forces of the West are so inferior to those of the Soviet Union that defeat is likely.

On the basis of population and industrial resources there is no physical reason why the states of Western Europe and Turkey shall not raise and maintain non-nuclear or so-called conventional forces comparable to those of the Soviet Union, even if we include in the enemy ranks the forces of the satellite states which I suppose are regarded as rather doubtful allies by the Russian general staff.

But the brutal fact must be faced that the democracies of West Europe whose population is approximately 200 millions are unwilling to make the effort to keep more than about 15 divisions in a state of readiness, whereas the Soviet Union has approximately 50 to 70 divisions more or less ready for action. It is because the governments of the West know that they cannot persuade their peoples to arm up conventionally to a figure approaching the Russian level that the issue is evaded by claiming that tactical nuclear weapons will redress the balance. It is also for this reason that in disarmament talks the West refuse to consider abandoning nuclear weapons unless there is also a reduction in conventional forces. To sum up:

In a major war with the Soviet Union we have said we have to use nuclear tactical weapons to make up for our shortage of conventional forces; the use of tactical nuclear weapons is almost certain to see-saw upwards to the largest nuclear weapons; against such weapons we cannot defend the United Kingdom. A defence strategy which is likely to lead to the use of a decisive weapon which will destroy what one is trying to defend cannot be commended, and the argument that our enemy will (we hope) later be destroyed is pointless. It is the basis of the argument of the deterrent that H-bomb warfare is so awful that neither side will use it if the other can retaliate in kind. If the nuclear deterrent works it will do so both after military operations start as well as before. But to use nuclear tactical weapons is to destroy the nuclear deterrent.

If nothing can be any worse than an H-bomb war we ought to make as sure as possible that it cannot happen. The only way to be fairly sure it *cannot* happen (as opposed to hoping one can deter the enemy) is not to have the H-bomb. This involves not having tactical nuclear weapons. This would mean having large conventional forces (in case the Soviet Union also does not use nuclear weapons) were it not for the fact these forces are useless if they were attacked nuclearly, which they certainly would be if the Soviet Union was losing the conventional war.

We are therefore obliged to recognize that our choice lies between being destroyed in an H-bomb war or accepting the notion that if we contract out of the use of nuclear energy for military purposes we are militarily defenceless against a power using nuclear weapons, and if not absolutely defenceless against the Soviet Union's conventional forces we are in a position of serious inferiority. However gallantly we fought there would always be the risk that the Soviet Union might quickly obtain military victory by giving her superior conventional forces the additional help of a few nuclear weapons.

The situation described above would be that in which the United Kingdom would find itself if we decided to abandon the idea based on the deterrent of the H-bomb. Another of "those harsh and inescapable facts" but not the same one as that mentioned by the Minister of Defence. We should have escaped from the fire of potential H-bomb destruction into the frying-pan of a potential occupation or, if not occupation, surrender to any demands put to us by the Soviet Government. Some will argue that although the fire is obviously hotter and more immediately fatal than the frying pan, the latter would be so unpleasant that there is not much to choose between immediate incineration and prolonged frying. But suppose we can find an idea which if we use it as the basis of our strategy of defence makes the frying-pan choice the key to victory? In that case there is everything to be said for the frying-pan. Moreover as we shall see there *is* such an idea and one which resolutely applied may well cause our enemies to see the danger to themselves of putting us in their frying-pan—or, as I shall show, getting into ours!

CHAPTER TEN

DEFENCE WITHOUT ARMS

IN THIS EXAMINATION of defence in the nuclear age we
are now through what I have called the thought barrier and in
a mental world which has hitherto been the exclusive area of
the Pacifist who asserts for moral reasons that it is the real
world. To non-Pacifists it has hitherto sounded like a visionary
world, but let non-Pacifists remember that without vision the
people perish!

I shall assume that the question as to whether the United
Kingdom should forswear the use of nuclear energy for military
purposes becomes a political issue in Britain and that the
electorate return to power a Government pledged to put this
policy into effect.

The first step would be consultation with our allies and, as
mentioned earlier, I estimate that the U.S.A. and Canada
(and possibly Australia) would not agree with our policy and
the two former powers would withdraw their forces certainly
from Great Britain, probably from Europe. On the other hand
France, Italy, Western Germany and the smaller western
powers might welcome our decision and be prepared to form
a new defence organization based on the principle of *non-use of
nuclear energy for military purposes*; a defence organization which
could be called the European Treaty Organization (E.T.O.).

The Continental powers have not (1957) reached the stage of
making their own nuclear weapons and, certainly in West
Germany and France, there is a very lively appreciation of the
fact that in a nuclear war their territories would be in the
target area. It has not escaped the notice of thoughtful Germans
that in the tactical atomic exercise carried out by Nato called
Carte blanche some 300 Hiroshima-sized atomic bombs were
theoretically dropped on West German territory.

To put the matter bluntly the Continental powers could do
no more than protest at our decision and it is certain that substantial sections of their populations would approve it. The

alternative open to these European nations would be an attempt to persuade the U.S.A. to continue to operate in a Nato of which Great Britain was no longer a member. It is not, of course, suggested, nor indeed would it be practical politics, that the U.K. should suddenly take and implement overnight the decision to abandon the use of nuclear energy for military purposes. The fact that this decision was being canvassed would explode a political atom bomb in the whole rather shaky structure of western defence arrangements as at present organized and cause a great deal of "agonizing appraisals".

There would be no reasons against and some for the idea that this decision once made, should be formally registered with the U.N. and that this body be invited to satisfy itself through an international inspectorate that the powers pledged not to use nuclear energy for military purposes were fulfilling this undertaking. The next decision the E.T.O. powers would have to take would be in connection with their conventional forces.

I have shown that theoretically and logically a decision to abandon the use of nuclear energy for military purposes leads to an abandonment of conventional forces intended to win a major war. But this is a matter of degree and to keep this decision within the bounds of practical politics, we should consider the situation of Switzerland.

This country is not protected by Nato and the deterrent and has no intention of getting under that umbrella. Yet it has armed forces (without, to the best of my belief, nuclear weapons) and I conceive the Swiss attitude to be as follows:

"We must accept the fact that if we are presented with an ultimatum from the Soviet Union or U.S.A. backed by the threat of an H-bomb attack we must accept its terms. But if we are faced with an attack by conventional weapons we will fight even though our resistance against the conventional forces of the Soviet Union could not be very prolonged (cf. the case of Finland)."

The European powers organized in a European Treaty Organization might decide that defence plans should be determined by the following principles or statements:

(1) That the strategy of defence of the E.T.O. powers be switched, so far as its main foundation is concerned, from a basis of armed force to one of political and moral force.

(2) That these political and moral forces as mentioned in Chapter VII would be organized for use in three operational theatres, viz.

> The home fronts
> The uncommitted nations' fronts
> The enemy fronts

(3) The object of the operations on the home fronts will be to create a sense of democratic unity amongst the E.T.O. peoples and also to train and prepare them for non-violent resistance in the event of an enemy occupation. Operations on the uncommitted nations' fronts will be designed to win those nations for the free way of life and encourage them to resist penetration by Communist ideology. Operations on the enemy fronts will have as their object the creation of pro-democratic opinion in the Soviet Union and satellite states.

(4) In addition to the establishment of an organization charged with applying democratic political and moral defence policies both domestically and internationally, E.T.O. states shall maintain conventional armed forces (non-nuclear) sufficiently large to maintain internal security.

(5) As an interim measure these conventional forces shall be large enough to provide a collective security force armed with non-nuclear arms of a size capable of putting up a token resistance to Russian non-nuclear armed aggression across E.T.O. frontiers.[1]

In a subsequent chapter I shall translate these general directives into suggested practices, but first I will consider some of the consequences which might flow from the adoption of such ideas as foundations of defence.

In considering this question I have made an estimate of Soviet intentions, which are usually and officially described as "world domination". I have never found this a very helpful definition; it is too vague. It is necessary to attempt a closer

---

[1] I would suggest a total E.T.O. force of about 10 divisions and corresponding air and sea forces. I believe it would gradually be reduced to a frontier guard.

appreciation of Soviet policy for which purpose two sources of evidence are available. They are what the Soviet leaders have said, and what they have done. They have said a great deal and what they have done is writ large in the history of our own times. I believe that Soviet policy is inspired by a mixture of motives, of which the following are the most significant:

(a) A motive of safeguarding the territorial integrity of the Russian homeland by ensuring that neighbouring states are controlled by Moscow. This is analogous to British determination for many years that no great power should control the Low Countries. In this part of the Russian policy is a fear that a united Germany might attack Russia. This is the defensive element in Russian policy and claims that the U.S.A. has encircled Russia with bases for nuclear attack. To this defensive part of Soviet policy should be added a strain of imperialist expansionist policy which has been characteristic of Russian policy for several centuries notably, for example, the Russian designs on Constantinople and expansion towards the Pacific now likely to be blocked by the emergence of Communist China.

(b) A motive based on a realization that in the world of to-day and especially of to-morrow there is not room for two ideologically opposed ways of life and if democracy is not destroyed it will destroy Communism. It is the policy of the Soviet leaders to attack and weaken by a great variety of methods, mostly political and economic, the democratic states and to bring uncommitted nations into the Communist alliance. This is the branch of Communist policy which includes sending arms to Arab states, encouraging foreign Communist parties, conducting world-wide propaganda, fomenting seditious movements and industrial unrest. These are some of the external manifestations of the second main motive in Soviet policy. It has an internal facet which is the efforts to raise the standards of living and productivity of the Soviet bloc so that its economic strength will enable it to out-do the capitalist world in material achievements. If this can be achieved the Soviet leaders will have the advantage of an impressive shop window displaying the benefits of Communism and they will also be able to use their surplus production for international political purposes in world markets.

If for example the Soviet Union were able to equal the economic strength of the U.S.A.—an ambition publicly proclaimed by Khrushchev—they could undertake some economic operations very embarrassing to the western world.

(c) A motive inspired by a genuine crusading spirit in some Soviet leaders, who believe that it is their mission to make a Communist world. How strong this is must be speculative. I find it hard to believe Stalin was a dedicated man and almost as hard to believe it of Khrushchev. There is little doubt that the genius Lenin[1] was such a man and Marshal Zhukov was said to be "an honest Communist" until November 1957 when Khrushchev sent a dog into outer space and the Marshal into outer darkness.

(d) A motive based on the lust for power. This cannot be exactly assessed, but on the testimony of the Communists themselves it was strong in Stalin's behaviour and may not be absent from Khrushchev's make-up and that of his enemies whom he recently overthrew. If democratic processes became established in Russia, the present rulers, with whom must be included all party members, would no longer occupy their privileged positions in the state. There is a powerful vested interest in Communism.

After studying the actions which have reflected these motives I conclude that the main idea in Soviet tactics is to proceed by non-violent methods wherever possible and that the use of violence is only looked upon in Moscow as needed in reserve to be used if all else fails. This analysis has the sanction of Lenin's opinion.

*　　　*　　　*

I now return to the question of: "What consequences would flow from the adoption by E.T.O. of the principles mentioned on page 147." The consequences will be considered under two headings, those which would be favourable and those which would be unfavourable.

From the favourable point of view we should achieve a great coup in the battle of the brains. Opinions will differ as to the

---

[1] "It would not matter one jot if three-quarters of the human race perished. The important thing is that the remaining quarter should be Communists"—Lenin writing to Maxim Gorki.

importance of world public opinion in general and in particular of its effect on the Soviet leaders.

The Soviet leaders attach much more importance to world public opinion than do democratic statesmen who are now beginning to discover its significance.

One of the most suggestive passages in General Sir Charles Keightley's despatch on the Suez operations was that: "*In modern days world public opinion is a most important weapon of war.*" Sir Charles ought to know about this and I suspect that he could expand that simple phrase into a book of startling revelations.

I believe that an announcement by Britain that (either unilaterally or with other European powers) she had abandoned the use of nuclear energy for military purposes and had done so as a calculated risk, would have a profound effect all over the world. It would restore her at one bound to that position of moral leadership she enjoyed during the nineteenth century when, we must not forget, she had behind that leadership an overwhelming naval strength. In those days the weapon of violence, if used, was moderate in its consequences. When in the nineteenth century Great Britain engaged in colonial wars she did not use a type of violence which obliterated the people with whom she was at war. The only way she could have produced in the nineteenth century the consequences of twentieth century nuclear violence would have been by massacring all the inhabitants in every colonial war.

To-day we must replace the gap left by the disappearance of the Pax Britannica, based on our overwhelming naval strength, by leadership based on overwhelming moral strength. A British decision (to abandon nuclear energy for military purposes) would, in some respects, seriously embarrass the Soviet Union whose escape route would presumably be as follows:

"We welcome this move by Britain which, as a peace-loving nation always fighting for peace, we should be happy to emulate, but unfortunately the U.S.A. has not seen fit to follow the enlightened British move and therefore, with the utmost regret the Soviet Union is obliged to continue its tests and stock-piling."

Notwithstanding this Russian excuse, the political warfare opportunities open to Britain in the Middle East and Asia would be greatly increased through our being able to say: "We had the Bomb and nuclear energy in other military forms and we have voluntarily given it all up. We are taking risks with our eyes open in order to give the world the historic lead needed to show humanity the way out of its present perils, and to demonstrate that nuclear energy shall only be used for peaceful purposes."

The next advantage would be economic. Our present direct annual expenditure on armaments being in the region of £1,500 million, to what would that be reduced to maintain conventional forces able to fulfil the principles listed on page 147?

To make this calculation one must fix a size for our conventional forces. This depends upon the extent to which conventional forces are needed in order to provide internal security and act as a frontier guard for the E.T.O. territories. As an approximate estimate—so far as the United Kingdom is concerned and allowing for a couple of airborne divisions for minor aggressions—I suggest the Royal Navy could be reduced to 30,000, the Army to 60,000 and the R.A.F. to 30,000 men. Civilian staffs directly employed might be cut to 50,000. These figures are probably much larger than are needed for the fulfilment of the E.T.O. principles.[1] Reductions of this character should produce direct savings of between £500 and £800 million a year and nearer the higher figure, bearing in mind that the conventional forces would not be armed with nuclear weapons or designed to undertake offensive operations in a major war. Apart from the direct savings there would be a large indirect saving of manpower and material which would have a profound effect on the economy of the country. For example a saving of £270 million enables a reduction of 1s. to be made in the income tax. But if a saving of £800 million were to be made on our present defence budget at least 50 per cent of this saving and perhaps more should still be allocated to defence. The sum of £400 million should be transferred to the budget of the Political Warfare activities of E.T.O. European powers, where savings comparable in percentages but less in volume to those in Britain would be made, would also have

[1] Captain Liddell Hart has suggested that by creating "New Model" divisions (equivalent in size to Russian divisions) a total force of 127,000 men would suffice for 2 Divisions in Germany, 1 at home, 1 in the Far East and 1 in the Eastern Mediterranean.

immense sums at their disposal for the three types of operation
mentioned in principles number two and three, i.e. the use of
political and moral forces on the three fronts.

*   *   *

We must now consider the disadvantageous consequences
which must be expected to flow from the new policy of abandoning the use of nuclear energy for military purposes.

First I would put a political result. It would mean a basic
disagreement between the United Kingdom and the U.S.A.
on ways and means of defence. Much would depend in the
first instance upon how the British policy were put across in
the U.S.A. but, if to abandon the use of nuclear energy for
military purposes is the correct policy and is so proved by
results, then the Americans will eventually come round to our
way of thinking.

There are great issues in the lives of men and nations when
decisions must be taken which cause many complications and
involve many risks and this would be such an issue and of a
magnitude unprecedented in the history of mankind. It would
be the claim of those who advocate that we should take this
bold step that it holds out a hope of reversing the trend of
history and dragging mankind back from the gulf which
yawns ahead, and for that a temporary estrangement from our
American friends is a small price to pay.

I have for many years preached the doctrine that Anglo-
American unity and co-operation must be the foundation of the
defence of the free world and harshly criticized, for example,
the refusal of the Americans in the post-World War II period to
concert a common policy with Great Britain in the Middle East,
the American independent policy in the Far East and the
British failure even to inform the Americans about the proposed
adventure in Egypt. The strenuous attempts which the Soviet
Union has made and continues to make to split America from
her allies is a tribute to the importance of this alliance. Nevertheless this alliance in the last analysis is a means to an end and
not an end in itself. Rightly or wrongly the American people
judged it to be in their best interest to remain neutral for a
long period in World War I, to withdraw into isolation for
some years after 1919 and to remain neutral again in 1939.

To-day this great nation has accepted the responsibilities of being the leader of the democratic world in the struggle of the cold war and has acted on the grand scale with economic and military aid.

But if we believe that circumstances have produced a situation in which the *methods* of the defence strategy of the West are erroneous it is our duty to argue our case with our American allies, endeavour to convert them and, if we are not successful, do what we believe to be right. I have expressed doubts whether the Americans (and Canadians) would go along with us but, although it would take us too far afield to foresee the course of the discussions between the U.K. and the U.S.A., it is possible that just as we have disagreed in a friendly manner on a question of principle in connection with the recognition of Communist China, so we could similarly agree to disagree on this much greater issue of the use of nuclear energy in war. I would say to my American friends: "Britain gave you a lead into violence which you followed in due course. Now we are giving you a lead into non-violence."

What might emerge from the negotiations would be a state of affairs in which the U.S.A. and the Soviet Union would face each other in the deadlock of a nuclear arms race and that the United Kingdom, the Western European states and the Asian and Middle East countries would share the common platform of being non-nuclear energy states for defence purposes.

What influence this non-nuclear group could exert to reduce tension between the two great nuclear powers cannot be foreseen, but on balance the existence of so great a body of world opinion in the non-nuclear camp, a body whose manifest self-interest was to assist in preventing a U.S.A.-Soviet nuclear war, seems better than the present state of affairs in which each of the chief opponents in the cold war is striving to draw the whole world into systems each of which depends for its defence on the nuclear weapon. I would like to make it clear that I am strongly opposed to the ideas of those who picture Great Britain as the centre of a third neutralist force armed with nuclear weapons. That idea embraces the worst of both worlds. Indeed I am strongly against neutralism (nuclear or otherwise) as a policy. We must remain solidly in support of the cause of freedom; but do so with a constructive strategy.

I come now to one of the most serious risks which would have to be faced as a consequence of the policy under discussion which is the possibility that it might lead to a Russian occupation of the E.T.O. territories. This could arise in various ways and I have selected one as being the most drastic. I can imagine the Soviet Union saying in effect: "The U.S.A. has decided to retain nuclear weapons. She has withdrawn from her bases in the United Kingdom and on the Continent but she still has bases in Iceland (perhaps), N. Africa and Arabia. It is necessary for the purpose of defending ourselves against U.S. aggression that we should have bases in Britain and in Western Europe. We demand that such bases be leased to the Soviet Union."

This would be a test case and there can be no doubt that the reply to the Soviet Union ought to be an indignant refusal.

The Soviet Union would then be faced with the following choice of action:

(*a*) Threaten to open up a nuclear attack on the West.
(*b*) Declare that it would move into Western Europe with conventional forces.
(*c*) Accept the rebuff.
(*d*) In the case of Britain, threaten or establish a naval blockade.

The choice before the Soviet Union would not be easy. Consider the threat to attack the West with nuclear weapons. It would have to be answered with the reply "Very well, you barbarians. Do it."

The Soviet Union might drop one bomb and, if they did so and were thus forced to translate what might have been bluff into action, we should have to say, before we were completely destroyed: "We accept your terms." But I do not believe that it would be practical politics for the Soviet Union leaders to make a nuclear attack on Britain simply because we refused to grant them bases. World opinion would be outraged and so would public opinion in the Red Empire. Others will say that Soviet public opinion does not count. It may not count for much yet, but it is counting for more than it did ten years ago and the main part of our defences, once we had abandoned nuclear energy, would be to make public opinion beyond the Iron Curtain more effective and informed.

In my opinion, therefore, it is unlikely that the Soviet Union would threaten or carry out course (*a*). But supposing they did? Are we any worse off for living under the threat of a token nuclear bombing than in our present (1957) position when, so far as one can estimate, we are going to be nuclear bombed in a big way before we "retaliate" on Russia if the deterrent fails to deter?

I come to course (*b*)—a conventional invasion. According to the E.T.O. principles this would meet with a token resistance and then we should be occupied, or have to concede the bases, and my view is that we should do our best to force the Soviet Union to undertake an occupation in order to get the bases. I deal with the problem of occupation in Chapter XII.

Coming now to the third case, where we suppose that the Soviet Union accepts the rebuff, this would be a signal and perhaps decisive victory for the West.

Searching around for other consequences disadvantageous to the West which might flow from our decision to abandon nuclear energy for military purposes, we come to the question of Russian expansion in various directions. It is impossible in a limited space to make a comprehensive list of the soft spots open to Russian aggression, but—at the moment of writing—Syria appears to be at the top of the list as a candidate for the first Soviet satellite[1] not linked by land to the Soviet Union. The significance of what is taking place in Syria to-day and may be in Iraq to-morrow and in Greece the day after to-morrow is that it is a form of Soviet aggression which is immune to military counter-attack.

The policy of military force has worked all right inside Syria as a support for political action; it is useless from outside in the hands of the West. Inside Syria a Communist political offensive supported at one remove by the Army has overthrown such democracy as existed. From outside Syria of what use is the American 6th Fleet perambulating in the Mediterranean with planes carrying H-bombs? None whatsoever, except to demonstrate that a Communist coup can take place under its bows. In what circumstances would there be any object in dropping an H-bomb on Damascus? None. Or what purpose, if troops were available (which they are not), of invading

[1] Excluding Albania and San Marino!

Syria? None. If we had no nuclear weapons we should be no more helpless than we are to-day to combat Russian designs on Syria by the use of force.

We need other methods, because what occurred in Syria in 1957 was an example of the classic Communist method of aggression by winning the battle of brains from within. Against this type of aggression armed force is useless.

Abandonment by the United Kingdom of the use of nuclear energy for military purposes (with all the further consequences I have mentioned) would release large resources for use in the only defence mechanism which can combat this type of aggressive policy, and that is various manifestations of political warfare. E.T.O. policy should make it more difficult for the Soviet leaders to pursue their traditional strategy because we shall be modernizing our defences and moving towards an era in which we should have got a jump ahead of the Communists in the conduct of war (werre), an activity in international relations in which armed force is becoming less and less valuable and more and more dangerous if used on a large scale.

Something must now be said of the special circumstances of the United Kingdom with regard to sea communications.

In the case of almost every nation in the world if an enemy (say the Soviet Union) made demands upon it and these demands were refused the enemy, in the last resort, had to move forward and occupy the territory of the nation which had refused the ultimatum. This was true before the arrival of the atomic weapon, but now a power possessing this weapon can destroy a state which has not got it and do so without the ·paraphernalia of an invasion. The atom bombs on Hiroshima and Nagasaki made it unnecessary for the American forces to carry out the costly operation of forcing their way into the main islands of Japan and the "invasion" became an unopposed occupation.

But the United Kingdom is a special case because a state wishing to bring overwhelming pressure on us if we had no armaments of any significance is not obliged either to come and occupy the Kingdom OR drop or threaten to drop an H-bomb on London. There is a third method of bringing pressure to bear on Britain which is a naval blockade. Whether our small conventional forces would make a token attack on the blockaders or test the reality of the blockade by risking a few ships would be decided according to the circumstances but I can imagine conditions in which it would be our correct strategy to resort to a strictly non-violent form of resistance and thus force the enemy either to threaten to bomb us or, failing this, occupy the United Kingdom.

This resistance would take the form of so organizing our defence arrangements that we could keep going for a long time without any exports or imports. "Keep going" need mean no more than keep alive at a bearable standard of life and the technical problem to be solved is stated in the following question:

"If storage plans are made and the indigenous resources of the nation organized on a national basis, for how long can 50,000,000 people in the United Kingdom maintain the basic needs of health?"

This is an enormous and interesting question beyond the scope of this book, but it ought to be looked into. My estimate is that it should not be too difficult to "keep going" for at least six months if the operation were well planned, including of course large stock-piling of wheat and other commodities; and possibly for 12 months.

It is a fascinating exercise of imagination to picture a besieged Britain living on its own resources, the centre of world attention, the miners performing prodigies of output, the agricultural community extracting every ounce of food from our soil, the whole nation on a basic food, fuel and clothing ration and basic wage, party politics forgotten and a renaissance of national purpose and unity far exceeding those stirring days (never to be forgotten by those who participated in them), when Great Britain stood alone after Dunkirk.

To this picture it is reasonable to add the trailer of a group of perplexed men in the Kremlin debating whether to use an H-bomb or send airborne divisions to resolve this unique and unprecedented development in defence against aggressive demands.

And in Washington? The President might be saying: "I have received an urgent message from the British Prime Minister stating that the whole nation is in excellent heart and that the plans prepared for this emergency are working well. Above all he urges most strongly that we should not start a nuclear war with the Soviet Union, but he would be glad if we would break off diplomatic relations with the Soviet Union and use our influence in all parts of the world to bring the maximum moral and economic pressure to the support of Britain. I have informed the British Prime Minister that at the appropriate moment, when this astonishing struggle ends, the British Government will be offered an outright gift in the shape of a credit for 5,000 million dollars.''

*   *   *

In case any reader should be asking himself whether some pages from a fictional book have been bound up by mistake in this volume, I ask him the following question:

Strange, extraordinary and incredible as may seem this picture of what-might-be, is it more out of the ordinary than would be a picture with an introduction which began: "It was at 0131 G.M.T. that the first H-bomb ever used in war exploded approximately 3 miles North of Piccadilly Circus. The shock of the explosion was felt throughout the S. Coast towns and the glare was observed at Liverpool . . ."?

*   *   *

A question which has sometimes been put to me is: "How would your proposals affect the question of Commonwealth defence and that of the colonies?" My short reply to that is as follows:

So far as Dominions are concerned the question of defending India, Pakistan, Ceylon, Australia, Canada, Malaya, South Africa, Ghana and New Zealand against attack with conventional forces by either China or the Soviet Union is not relevant for the simple reason that we have not the resources to defend them except in a subsidiary manner. Canada in all respects, and Australia and New Zealand in most, now look to the U.S.A. South Africa does not rely on Britain for her defence and the most likely crisis there is an internal one in which British force could play no part.

The fall of Singapore rang down the curtain on the era during which the people of an island in the North Sea could exercise military might East of Suez. The evacuation of the Canal Zone was a later episode in the great retreat.

So far as the colonial territories are concerned the chief problem is the possibility that force may be needed for the maintenance of internal security and this would be available in the shape of the highly mobile limited conventional forces which I propose should be maintained for non-global, non-nuclear military action against small-scale aggressions and riotous commotions.

In the case, for example of Hong Kong it is fantastic nonsense to suppose that we could defend it against a large-scale Chinese attack, or that we could help S.E. Asia, including Malaya, if the Chinese decided one day to expand their territories by military aggression.

From the military point of view "bases" in places like Gibraltar, Malta, Cyprus, Aden, Singapore and Hong Kong are rapidly becoming useless in nuclear war. The fixed base whose latitude and longitude is known exactly is the rocketeer's dream target.

CHAPTER ELEVEN

E.T.O. IN ACTION

THE FUNCTIONS of the European Treaty Organization (which would consist of those Western European nations as are willing to go along with Britain[1] in her abandonment of the use of nuclear energy for military purposes) would be derived from the five statements set forth on page 147, Chapter X.

One of the jobs to be done on the home front (see statement two) would be the preparation and training of the nations to deal with an enemy occupation. I shall put this important question aside for the moment and deal with it in Chapter XIV.

The other job to be done on the home fronts is educational work to show the peoples of the E.T.O. nations that they share in essential features a common way of life, which they are determined to defend notwithstanding their abandonment of nuclear energy for military purposes.

The ordinary elector is not interested in abstractions, but he can be interested in institutions. With the exception of Portugal, and to some extent Turkey, all the European Nato peoples (who for my present purpose can be regarded as belonging to the potential home front of E.T.O.) have institutions common to, and essential to their way of life, and certain to disappear if Communist ideas prevailed. In this short study I must limit myself to choosing two important examples; the institution of Parliament and the institution of the free Press.

There is in existence, and has been for seventy years, the Inter-Parliamentary Union, a body composed of legislators from the Parliaments of the world. It was created in 1887

---

[1] If the U.S.A., Canada and other non-European states decided to follow the British lead, so much the better. But I have thought it more realistic to assume they would not do so. The Asian states might form A.T.O. (Asian Treaty Organization) which could co-operate with E.T.O. The Asian Dominions would certainly approve of the British initiative.

when it never occurred to anyone that a democratic form of parliamentary government was not the ideal. For decades the I.P.U. has been a social gathering of legislators, though of recent years there have been signs of a realization that the I.P.U. could also be a serious body for the improvement of parliamentary government. But also of recent years this body has admitted to its ranks the "Parliamentarians" from the Communist parliaments! There is evidence that the Communists, following their usual tactics, are out to capture the I.P.U. and turn it into a Communist front. They are not—I hope—likely to succeed, but nor do I see much sign that the democratic members of the I.P.U. realize the political warfare value of the I.P.U. and that it ought to be used by them (now that they have admitted the enemy to their councils) as a political warfare battlefield with Communists.

There is also the Hansard Society for Parliamentary Government, an unofficial body with a small income from donations. Within the limits of its resources it does do exactly what could and should be done on a larger scale. For example, it has recently carried out a campaign in British schools to spread information about the American system of representative government and the Society would like to carry out projects such as that put forward to the Secretary-General of Nato in 1954. It was that, when a man is called up for national service in any Nato country, he should be given a small booklet of about 12 pages explaining in simple terms that he was not *only* being called up to defend his country, but also had the responsibility of defending the free way of life in all the Nato countries, which included *inter alia* free elections. The booklet would then explain the importance of the vote and be illustrated with pictures of elections in the Nato countries. It was estimated this job could be done for about £50,000-£75,000 but at that time the total budget in Nato for activities under Article II was £30,000!

This is one small example of the innumerable methods by which educational work could and should be done to build up a sense of "*belonging to the free world*". Another proposal also put forward by the Society was that the Speakers of the free parliaments should meet at bi-annual conferences and that these events could be used to illustrate and emphasize the

F

importance to all Nato countries of the institution of Parliament. If the Hansard Society were endowed it would set up a Parliament House with a permanent exhibition, etc., as a world centre of study and educational work about the institution of parliamentary government and its importance in the practice of the democratic way of life.

The free Press was mentioned above as an institution common to the free countries, which would disappear if the Communist creed prevailed. The newspaper proprietors of the free countries should get together and organize a large mobile exhibition showing people the difference between the free Press and a totalitarian Press.

These examples illustrate some of the many ways in which a climate of opinion could be created favourable to the idea that we all "belong" to a democratic brotherhood and that to create and strengthen this sense of unity in support of a menaced cause would add substantially to our psychological defence potential. The story of the past ten years shows practically no sign that this aspect of defence has ever been seriously considered by the leaders of the West.

A typical illustration of this neglect is the story of United Europe since the idea was first revived by Sir Winston Churchill soon after World War II. The present writer was one of the original Committee of twelve formed in Britain and has seen the whole story from within. It is a sad story, and the record of successive British governments who threw away an unique opportunity to give a great lead to the western world is not a creditable page in our history. Particularly distressing was the fact that Sir Winston, who had done more than any other man to give life to the idea, abandoned it at the behest of its enemies in the Tory Party when he became Prime Minister. This caused sardonic delight amongst the Socialists who had never seen any contradiction between their opposition to United Europe and their claims to represent to a particularly refined extent the doctrine of the brotherhood of man.

If in the 1950's under vigorous leadership from Britain a true United Europe had begun to take shape—and there was a moment when it looked as if the Council of Europe was the foundation of a growing edifice—this achievement would have been a powerful weapon in the political war against the Soviet Union, for it would have shown that the western nations were prepared to apply to their international relationships the principles of democracy on which they based their domestic arrangements and which they claimed they were defending against Communism.

It is never too late to reform and all these suggestions could be included even in our present defence schemes. Therefore I urge that without delay a large-scale and serious effort be made by Nato governments, as part of our defences against the Soviet political warfare, to build up a democratic psychological front using for this purpose Article II of the Nato Treaty and the Brussels Treaty. The building up of United Europe, politically, economically (free trade area and common market)[1] and culturally (abolition of passports to facilitate travel), should be regarded as a task of importance to defence.

The Council of Europe, it is good to report, is making plans to have exhibits at the 1958 Brussels Universal and International Exhibition: "designed to bring home to the public all that it owes to democratic institutions. Only too often disillusioned remarks are made by those who have already forgotten the evil deeds and crimes of the dictatorships . . . the display will show how primitive man, whose only law was brute force, has gradually progressed from tribal and local meetings through regional, provincial and national assemblies to the level of international and supra-national assemblies."

Efforts of all kinds must be made to create the same spirit of co-operation between the peoples of the western world in the non-military sphere as that which has been achieved between the military forces of the West. All this would be the task of E.T.O. on the home fronts and its slogan should be "It is not enough to believe in democracy, it must be practised internationally."

The second theatre of operations mentioned in the task of E.T.O. concerned the uncommitted nations. It would be one of the tasks of E.T.O. to use a large part of the savings made by the reduction of the armaments of its members for technical

---

[1] The British, having dragged their feet for years over United Europe, suddenly discovered that six European powers had managed to agree on a common market treaty and that Britain was on the doorstep! Hence the quick conversion to the merits of the free trade area.

assistance to underdeveloped non-committed nations and *ask for nothing in exchange*. The approach should be inspired by the spirit of: "It is our privilege and duty as democratic peoples to offer you assistance. You are astonished we do not seek concessions or lay down conditions? That may be the Communist way (openly or covertly), it is not our way of life. Indeed if it comes to our knowledge that there is famine in Communist China we should regard it as our duty to offer food unconditionally."

Although too long to quote in full, there appeared an excellent letter in *The Times* of 3rd September, 1957 by a Mr. Ballantyne pointing out (in regard to British influence in the Persian Gulf) "that policies that were adequate when we were able by strength to dominate and dictate have been proved worse than useless"—he went on to ask for "positive proof that we are prepared to work with the Arabs as friends and partners . . . to give assistance or advice when asked for it in their interests and not our own".

The object of the whole operation should be to win the battle of the brains in the struggle with the Soviet Union for the respect and mental allegiance of the peoples of the uncommitted nations. To do this we must not only talk democracy but practise it.

In his presidential address at the 1957 meeting of the British Association for the Advancement of Science, Professor P. M. S. Blackett pointed out that 400,000,000 people in the West have an annual income of about £200-£300 per head and that, (excluding China) there are 1,000,000,000 people in Asia, Africa and S. America with an average annual income of £20 per head. He further remarked that "the western world is saving and investing productively some £30 per head in plant and machinery to create more wealth . . . the West is thus saving more per head than the East is spending on everything. . . ."

In India, even if the ambitious plans for development can be sustained, "half a century would elapse before the standard of living in India would climb from one-tenth to one-fifth of that of Europe". Professor Blackett suggested that the west should make a free annual gift of 1 per cent of their income to the underdeveloped nations. This would amount to £1,000,000,000 of which the British share would be £150,000,000 or approximately 10 per cent of the present annual direct expenditure on armaments. It has been Soviet policy to claim that they give "aid without strings" (at any rate visible strings!) and when the Soviet leaders succeed in raising Russian productivity we shall find them using this economic weapon more and more as a means of Soviet penetration into uncommitted areas.

There would be psychological advantage in donating to underdeveloped nations nuclear power stations and explaining that these gifts were related to our decision not to use nuclear energy for military purposes.

The third and perhaps most important of three fields in which the political warfare defence programme of E.T.O. would operate is the attack on public opinion in the Communist states. This is the section of the field of political warfare where recognition of its significance as a weapon of defence has made the most progress since 1945.

We have moved forward from the ante-deluvian notion that nothing should be done to try to weaken the hold of governments on the minds of their peoples until military operations began or even after the shooting started. It is only forty years since there occurred the comic case of the cartoon dropped by aircraft over the German lines. This leaflet showed a picture of the Kaiser and his sons in uniform and bore the caption: "A German family that has had no losses in the War." The Germans objected to this on the grounds that its distribution was an offence against military discipline and threatened severe penalties against airmen captured distributing this propaganda! After an attempt to distinguish between inflammatory and non-inflammatory propaganda, the British War Office gave in over this matter.

Today, both from official and unofficial sources efforts are made to penetrate the psychological Iron Curtain with information about the free world and arguments are put up intended to change the minds of the peoples in the Communist-ruled states or at any rate give them ideas likely to weaken their support of the régime. Broadcasting is the chief method employed and the proof that the pudding is eaten is the refusal of the Communists to abandon jamming of western broadcasts.

My criticism of the western offensive in this department of

the war is that the psychological attack of the democracies on the minds of the peoples beyond the Iron Curtain is still only regarded as a minor and unimportant part of our defence arrangements. In Britain the highest level it reaches in the ministerial hierarchy is that of a junior Minister. Yet in para 3 of the 1956 Statement on Defence it is declared that "peace and prosperity within which the peoples of the world can develop their lives in freedom" . . . depend upon the arrival of *"such time as a true understanding of western policies can make its impact on the Soviet people."*

This is an important truth and one might have expected the Defence Statement to elaborate how much money was going to be spent and what methods would be used to ensure that "a true understanding" made "its impact on the Soviet people". But the subject is never again mentioned.

Professor Seton-Watson wrote (in *The Spectator*) on 23rd August, 1957 in connection with the Russian service of the B.B.C.

"Presentation of Britain is important . . . but there is a third task: to discuss in terms intelligible to Soviet citizens, the problems of society and politics which affect them in their daily life in the Soviet Union . . . young Soviet citizens are passionately, critically and intelligently interested both in the reality of their own society and in what the west thinks about it. Intelligent discussion of Soviet social problems, intelligent comment on Soviet political affairs which are excluded from the Soviet Press have a potential audience in the Soviet Union . . . the last thing we want is ranting propaganda . . . if it be true that the best hope of national, or even physical, survival for the people of Britain in the next twenty years lies in the movement of Soviet society away from the totalitarian imperialism of the dead Stalin and the living Khrushchev, it is equally true that such movement depends far more on the people of the Soviet Union than on western broadcasting. Nevertheless, the injection of ideas from outside, though it cannot create the movement,[1] can accelerate it. If a politically-minded intelligent and sophisticated B.B.C.'s Russian Service could accelerate it by 1 per cent, it would be worth a good many aircraft and divisions. I hope, Sir, that neither the silence of

[1] Why? Action starts from an idea. S.K.-H.

the Russian Service nor the indifference of our politicians will deter you from your admirable efforts to cast light on this dark corner of our national defence."

Illustrations have already been given in Chapter VIII of what is meant by political warfare operations against the enemy ideas and, in replacement of the meagre and somewhat disjointed psychological activities which are part of our present defence arrangements, I ask for a really powerful E.T.O. assault on the minds of the people behind the Iron Curtain, an assault adhering strictly to sound democratic principles and the truth.

In such an assault E.T.O. would have two great advantages. First it would have the good ideas and the good ideas can be as mentally destructive of bad ones as an H-bomb can be materially destructive. Great is the power of ideas! Who can assess the influence on world history of ideas which came from the minds of Jesus and the great religious teachers, or Lenin the materialist? It is our faith that we have the right ideas and in the long run Truth will prevail, but no harm is done in helping it to spread and this would be the second advantage enjoyed by E.T.O., for it would have all the resources needed in manpower and money.

It has been suggested that E.T.O. would maintain small conventional forces whose purpose would be to provide a trip wire and put the Soviet Union psychologically in the wrong if they attempted non-nuclear armed aggression across frontiers. The E.T.O. conventional force should also be so organized that it could at immediate notice produce an airborne force to be known as the *Rescue Division*. This body, largely composed of technical services, would be sent by the E.T.O. Council to any part of the world which had suffered a great national disaster, e.g. floods, earthquakes, famine, disease, etc. It would be at the disposal through U.N. channels of any state (Communist or non-Communist) which requested its help in an emergency and *there would be no charge for its services*, which would be regarded as the practical application of democratic principles. It would be the duty of E.T.O. to maintain this force as an E.T.O. body and, although to begin with the question of internal security would continue no doubt to be regarded as a reserved subject in the field of national sovereignty and therefore the national contingents of the E.T.O. force would operate independently in this respect, this should only be for a transitional period. As E.T.O. developed an ever-closer political and economic co-operation between its members it would become obvious that the internal security of each member-state was a matter of common concern.

Even in Nato as it exists to-day it is a manifest absurdity that the struggle in Algeria, or Cyprus (or the Suez adventure) are all labelled national problems with which other members of Nato are not supposed to be concerned, although the effectiveness of Nato is in fact closely affected by such questions. This contradiction is a great handicap to the Nato powers in any campaign of political warfare against the monolithic Soviet bloc.

The improvements in democratic co-operation which it would be the duty of E.T.O. to promote and assist have been suggested as defence measures linked with the assumption that the E.T.O. powers were non-nuclear states. Even if the menace of international Communism did not exist, these extensions into international life of democratic practices are an essential political development if mankind is to remain the master of his scientific achievements.

"Nato"—a Cabinet Minister told me—"is the child of fear." He might have said with equal truth "it was the child of Stalin". He went on to suggest that most progress comes about through fear of the consequences of not moving forward; he was a man of much experience in government.

Accepting—regretfully so far as this author is concerned—the theory that *fear* is a dominating motive in men's actions, one can argue that *fear* of nuclear war may make some states abandon nuclear energy for military purposes and that *fear* of the consequences of this decision may make them come together to concert the alternative means of defence and in doing so learn the reality of the brotherhood of man.

PART THREE

INTRODUCTION TO PART THREE

"WHAT'S HAPPENING on the other side of the hill?" is a question the skilful military commander keeps well in mind and to which his intelligence staff are ceaselessly endeavouring to find the answer.

It is a fact that as a rule subsequent revelations show that the general tendency is always to over-rate the power of the enemy and under-rate the difficulties which he is experiencing "on the other side of the hill". For example, we now know that in 1914 the German General Staff had an exaggerated idea of the offensive capabilities of the British Navy and imposed an unnecessarily timid policy on the High Seas Fleet. We know to-day that in the early months of the Second World War the German Army in the West was much thinner on the ground than we supposed it to be. We also know to-day that in terms of actual operation the much-feared German invasion of Britain in 1940 never advanced further than the first planning and also that the Germans were not aware how perilously low our fighter aircraft strength was towards the end of the Battle of Britain.

In Chapter X something was said about the possible courses of action open to the Soviet Union if Great Britain (either alone or in co-operation with other western powers) adopted the policy of abandoning the use of nuclear energy for military purposes, but my present purpose is to make an assessment of the extent to which I believe this policy would create grave difficulties for the Soviet leaders in the carrying out of their long-term strategy.

I start with an assumption, shared by all those who have made a close study of Communism, that the basis of their strategy is ideological. It is a profound error to suppose that the kind of world domination they are seeking to obtain is analogous to that of the Empires of the past such as the conquests of Alexander the Great, the Persian Emperors, the Romans, or—(with some reservations) Napoleon Bonaparte, the Kaiser's Germany, Hitler or the British Imperialism in its

pre-Boer War manifestation. If a parallel is to be sought from
the past, seek it in the Mohammedan offensive against the
Christian world; but the truth is that the Communist offensive
is something new in history although this is not to deny that in
it are to be found elements of the nineteenth-century Russian
Imperialism—but this is not the dominant element.

It will illustrate my conception of the nature of the Communist policy if we take note of the fact that all over the
world there are people who criticize what they regard as the
undesirable penetration into their natural cultures of various
manifestations of what is called "the American way of life".
I am not arguing whether certain American materialistic
interpretations of the western way of life are good or bad, but
that what is sometimes called *Coca-Colaism* has spread all over
the world, is a fact.

If one can imagine that it were the policy of the American
Government to use every possible method to Americanize the
world (including the threat of force), and that the American
people supported this policy because they sincerely believed
(and those who doubted it were suppressed) that the rest of
the world, if not Americanized, would be able to fulfil an
ambition of destroying the American way of life *in America*,
then I think we have a picture illustrative of Russian policy.

The Communist leaders must have behind them, if their
policy is to be effective, the support of the mass of the Russian
people and, in order to retain their support, it is essential for
the Soviet leaders to be able to persuade the Russian people of
three things:

First, that the Communist régime in Russia, with its present
hardships (e.g. great shortage of housing, indifferent standard
of living) is the only road to better conditions in the future.

Second, that Russia is surrounded by wicked capitalist
powers who are jealous and afraid of the wonders achieved by
the Communists and would like to bring them all down in
ruin. From this catastrophe the Russian people are protected
by the wisdom, energies and devotion of the Communist Party.

Third, that apart from the domestic importance of Communism to the welfare of the Russian people, the C.P. is also
engaged—on behalf of the Russian people—in a great mission-
ary task to rescue colonial and backward peoples from the

tyrannies of the Imperialists. Some authorities believe there is a messianic strain in the Russian character. (cf. The American dream. See page 51.)

It is essential, if these three ideas are to make sense to a Russian public opinion, which is rapidly becoming better educated in a technical sense, *that an atmosphere of crisis be maintained.*

"Peaceful co-existence" is a double-talk slogan. Tensional co-existence is what the Communists must have to maintain the climate of a struggle. There must be the "fight" for peace; the "battle" of the virgin lands; the class-struggle and so forth.

The adoption by the E.T.O. powers of non-violent resistance as a basis for defence would make it much harder for the Soviet leaders to maintain the *essential tensions* between Russia and the West European powers.

The most difficult of all the problems which face the Russian leaders is how on the one hand to educate their people, raise their standards of living, etc., and yet keep them mentally monolithic. It is our business to do all we can to make this insoluble problem burst wide open at the earliest possible date.

It is my belief that the adoption of the policy outlined in this book, when viewed from all angles, would be regarded by the Communist leaders as a master stroke of political warfare likely to do enormous damage to the hold of the Communist Party on the Russian people.

A radical change in the basis of our defence policy would not alter the fundamental nature of the "war" between Communism and Democracy, but it would profoundly change its character by transferring the centre of gravity of the difference between the two ways of life from the sphere of violence to that of ideas. If this could be achieved the Soviet leaders would have to decide whether they would openly declare that it was their intention to use their superior force physically to occupy Western Europe, the Middle East and perhaps some Asian countries by force.[1] I believe that it would be impossible for them to follow this policy and retain the essential support of the Russian people. On the contrary, my supposition is that the Soviet leaders' reaction, realizing the extreme dangers to their whole strategy of the move of the E.T.O. powers to contract

[1] The Chinese might have something to say about this.

out of violence as a means of attack and defence, could be epitomized in the following assessment which I have taken the liberty of attributing to Khrushchev at a meeting of the Presidium:

"Comrades, we all know that J. V. Stalin committed a grievous error by putting so much emphasis on the element of force in our over-all strategy. This had the serious effect of so alarming our enemies that they overcame their internal contradictions sufficiently to create Nato and even bring the Germans into it. Now we are faced with a most dangerous development in which a substantial section of the Western world has contracted out of the use of force. We are left in the posture of a boxer whose opponent had slipped under the ropes and left the ring.

"Fortunately, most fortunately, the U.S.A. has remained in the atomic ring, otherwise the situation would be catastrophic. As Stalin was to the Western World, so are the Americans to us—the provider of the essential of fear which will enable us to maintain the climate of crisis."

What *would* happen on the other side of the hill in the Kremlin (and beyond the Iron Curtain) is speculative but what has been happening since the famous denunciation of Stalin is as clear as daylight. There is a ferment of ideas amongst the intellectuals. Heretical books explode like tactical nuclear weapons, there is tension amongst the leaders and a mass of evidence that the "home front" all over the Communist world is in a sensitive and politically active condition and seeking the mirage of a reformed and more libertarian expression of Communism. Most important, Moscow has lost its monopoly as the only centre of Communist dogma. This presents the democratic world with a great opportunity, and to change the basis of our defence policy as suggested in this book is the best way to exploit and make fatal the dilemma of our mortal enemies.

CHAPTER TWELVE

PROBLEMS OF OCCUPATION

IT WAS MENTIONED on page 141 that the people of the United Kingdom during the past five or six hundred years have not shared with the majority of mankind a realization that the occupation by enemy forces of a people's homeland is an event which may occur once in a generation.

The British, secure behind their moat and guarded by a powerful fleet, thought of the act of invasion as a phenomenon from which they were immune. They were the invaders; never the invaded.[1]

In 1940 this attitude changed almost over-night as the British were warned by their Government that an invasion by the German army might at any moment be launched. We now know that this attack was never so imminent as was thought at the time and up to date (1957) the United Kingdom still holds what must be a world record in freedom from invasion period.

It has also been stated that one of the consequences of changing the basis of our defence strategy from material force to moral and psychological forces would be that in certain circumstances it would not be possible to deny our enemy access to the Kingdom and that this event would—in the new defence arrangements—have to be considered as a continuation of the battle and not the end of the war.

Before examining some of the problems—from both sides— of an occupation the reader must be reminded that in terms of conventional warfare the United Kingdom is more liable to invasion to-day than at any previous period in her history; a fact of present-day life which has nothing to do with any question of changing the basis of our defence strategy.

No one knows whether the H-bomb will continue to deter:

[1] "We fight our wars in other peoples' countries. France, the Low Countries, Germany, the Crimea, Africa, India, the Pacific and so on. We prefer it that way. It is inconvenient when you have to fight in your own country." (Field Marshal Viscount Montgomery, 21st October, 1957).

whether if it does not, strategic nuclear weapons will be used in the opening stages of a third world war, or whether there would be a period of "phoney war" (in nuclear terms) during which neither side would initiate nuclear strategic bombing but only use tactical nuclear weapons.[1] Therefore, one of the contingencies for which we must prepare is a struggle between conventional forces using tactical nuclear weapons so far as possible strictly for military purposes, i.e. attacks on enemy formations, military bases, ports, airfields, etc. The forces of the Soviet Union for this type of semi-nuclear war are superior to those of the Democracies.[2] The prospects of preventing the Soviet forces from reaching the Atlantic seaboard are not comforting and, with Western Europe in their grip, an invasion—possibly airborne—of the U.K., supported by a massive submarine attack and air-bombing with tactical nuclear weapons, is something we should take into account in our existing defence plans. Only wishful thinking will assume that such an invasion is bound to be repulsed.

In short, even if the policy of abandoning the use of nuclear energy for military purposes is rejected out of hand, I ask the question: "As matters stand, what plans exist to cope with the contingency of an enemy occupation of the U.K.?" Some say that it would be a mistake to have such plans. They base this opinion on two arguments:

(a) As such plans would have to be made known to the public it would lower national morale if it seemed that the Government were not certain an invasion could be repulsed.

(b) Preparation of plans to meet an occupation (not the same thing as plans to repel an invasion) is senseless because if the United Kingdom were occupied, the war—so far as Britain is concerned—is lost, and we could only hope to be liberated.

The validity of these arguments depends on (b) and this depends upon whether or not the thesis put forward in this book about what—in the last resort—we are defending is

---

[1] The near-certainty that this policy would build up into H-bomb operations is discussed on page 106.
[2] The Soviet Union are believed to have ten airborne divisions (1957).

accepted. This thesis is that in the final analysis we are defending our way of life and fundamentally the *ideas* which give immortality to our way of life.

If this objective be accepted, then to believe that an enemy occupation of these islands is the end of the struggle is defeatism; it is treachery to democracy. People who think like this should think again and desert from the mental fifth column.

If this objective is not accepted, there is no more to be said except to ask the materialists what military plans they have to ensure that an occupation of the U.K. is a virtual impossibility. The only answer they can produce is—paradoxically—the *idea* of the deterrent of the H-bomb since there are no signs that the British or any other nation of the West are prepared to raise and maintain conventional forces at least as strong as, and preferably stronger than, those of the Soviet Union as an insurance policy in case H-bombs are not used. Our weakness in conventional forces is particularly noticeable in relation to the Russian submarine menace.[1]

The sinister implications of nuclear war seem to have caused everyone except professional sailors to overlook the fact that, even if we assume no one will use nuclear weapons, Great Britain, dependent for her normal existence upon sea communications, is rapidly becoming most gravely menaced by the Soviet submarine fleet, whose activities would be supplemented by conventional bombing activity and air-minelaying against our ports. To this we must add bombardment of our ports by intermediate rockets. My view is that with modern weapons (non-nuclear if you like) the United Kingdom is virtually indefensible if powerful Russian forces were established on the Atlantic sea-board and 400 plus Russian submarines were operating in the Western Approaches.

* * *

No plans exist to meet the contingency of an enemy occupation, for if they did they would have to be published. If I am wrong and they exist in a safe, they are useless whilst secret. Plans—probably of an embryonic character—may exist to deal with repelling an invasion but this is not the same thing.

It would be interesting if personalities such as the Governor

[1] See Chapter VI, page 89.

of the Bank, the Chairmen of the Big Five, the President of the
T.U.C., the Archbishop of Canterbury, the Editor of *The Times*,
the Director-General of the B.B.C., the Chairman of I.C.I. and
the Chairmen of a couple of nationalized industries appeared
in a television series and answered three questions:

(1) Have you had an indication from the Cabinet about
what policy you are to pursue if this country is invaded and we
fail to repel the attack so that we are occupied?

(2) If the answer is in the negative, what ideas have *you* got
as to the policy *you* would pursue?

(3) If you *have* some ideas, what steps have you taken to
make them known in the organization of which you are the
chief personality?

I feel that the programmes would be brief and embarrassing
to performers and viewers.

Even if no attention is paid to the possibility of basing our
defence on the alternative to discarding nuclear energy for
military purposes, the absence of any plan to meet an occupation under any circumstances is a weakness in our defences.

II

The problems of an occupation which might be one of the
consequences of the new strategy need examining, for it would
not be a normal or traditional type of occupation because it
would not be preceded by great or prolonged violence. In
World War II four cases of occupation which were of this
character come to mind. One was the negotiated occupation of
Iceland by the Allies; another was the German occupation of
Denmark (preceded by slight armed resistance) and the third,
a somewhat exceptional case, the extension of the German
occupation to the Southern half of France. The fourth was the
occupation of the Channel Islands.[1]

Although the U.K. came no nearer to being occupied than
being threatened with invasion, it is of some interest to see what

[1] There was some criticism in the U.K. of what was regarded as the collabora-
tionist attitude of some Channel Island residents. This does not seem to have
affected post-war popularity of the islands as a tourist resort or bolt-hole from
British income and sur-tax. One of my constituents said: "Eh lad! Bad news to-
day. Bloody Channel Islands liberated." He was a grower of tomatoes.

plans existed for each contingency—bearing in mind that it would have been an occupation *after* resistance—they ranged from the purely comic to the ludicrous.

In his book *Invasion 1940*[1] Mr. Peter Fleming has some information which indicates that plans for the conduct of civilians were amateurish and belonged to the anti-invasion plans and not to the possible post-invasion or occupation period. The same author collected information from the German archives about what the Nazis intended to do with an occupied Britain. The result of his researches are that: "no clear picture survives of how they proposed to govern the U.K. after they had subdued it" and Mr. Fleming could only find some rather slapdash plans for military government during the invasion period.

From conversations with officials such as Chief Constables, who realized in 1940 that they might be faced with an occupation problem, I conclude: that no instructions were received from Whitehall on this matter; that at the local or regional level some took the view that the Police, as members of the civilian population, should accept the invasion and do what they could to assist the German authorities in the maintenance of law and order; others decided to go "underground" and told their men they could do what they liked. One senior officer who had decided to go "underground" informed me that: "I told the older constables who were in villages that it was probable that they would not be arrested by the Germans as they would be required to act as police officers on their behalf. This was what I believe happened in the Channel Islands." The available evidence indicates that on both sides there was very little planning or thinking concerned with the situation after the fighting had ceased due to a German military victory.

The same answer applies to the question "Did the West European governments have any plans for how to deal with a possible German occupation?" The case of France provides plenty of evidence that there were no plans. As the victorious armies pressed forward, members of the French Government sat in Bordeaux disputing amongst themselves whether or not the seat of government should be transferred to N. Africa, a reasonable move which should have been planned at the latest

[1] *Invasion 1940* by Peter Fleming. Rupert Hart-Davis.

during the months of the phoney war. Nothing illustrates more dramatically the absence of any planning, than the amazing *ad hoc* offer by the British Government of complete union with France, an idea which, according to information given to me by one of its authors, was very much an off-the-cuff decision.

From the point of view of the occupying powers the most complete study which has come to my notice has been written by Mr. A. Dallin. His book[1] is a huge volume of nearly 700 pages, weightily documented and an astonishing revelation of the internal rivalries in the Nazi party and between the army and the party, which led (in addition to fearful brutalities) to a hotch-potch of contradictory policies often simultaneously applied. This book also shows that the Nazis had a tremendous chance to win over the support of a population which in the Ukraine and elsewhere first welcomed the German army as liberators.[2] Most interesting from the point of view of our present purpose is the evidence in this book that it is impossible to get any profit out of an occupied country without the assistance of the inhabitants and that, however brutal and indifferent to any moral considerations the occupiers may be, in the long run they have to take account of some of the desires and wishes of the occupied people.

When the Allies occupied West Germany after the enemy had unconditionally surrendered, although the leading Nazis were seized and tried as criminals, the occupying powers were obliged, *faute de mieux*, to make use of many former Nazi officials so that the administration could function and order be brought out of chaos.

The two difficulties which the occupying authorities have to surmount are first, the need to keep the economic life of the conquered territories in working order if the conquerors are to acquire any economic benefit, and the more complex the society of the occupied people, the less easy it is to impose some rough and ready alien administration without the whole apparatus breaking down.

The second problem facing an occupier is of recent origin.

---

[1] *German Rule in Russia 1941-45* (a study of occupation policies). Macmillan.
[2] "We are enthusiastically welcomed on all sides" (July 1941). "The basic attitude is one of deep resignation" (August 1942). "In truth the bulk of the population is hostile" (October 1943). Extracts from German intelligence reports.

It has been considered in the past that if a state were invaded and occupied, this event marked the end of the war and that the nation as represented by its government had no option but to capitulate and accept the terms of a "peace" settlement, which might amount to annexation of the conquered territory. This, however, was a short-term view because there are many examples in history which show that military defeat, occupation and annexation did not result in the disappearance of the nation and its way of life. A classic example is provided by Poland, frequently partitioned and eventually abolished as a state. It was resurrected in 1919, passed under Russian control again after World War II and at the time of writing is endeavouring to regain a measure of independence. Eire, Czechoslovakia, Finland—and Israel—are also examples of the indestructibility of national ways of life. The history of China—which in the past has been a civilization rather than a nation—is often the story of how the Chinese absorbed their conquerors.

That there is nothing new in the idea that all is not lost if the homeland is occupied or even annexed, is an oversimplification, but during the past few decades the application of the principle has taken on a significant new development.

In the past a state which occupied another could expect a certain amount of underground resistance which, if the occupation became an annexation, was reflected in an independence movement usually centred in refugee groups operating from a neutral territory. The United Kingdom, with its tradition of political freedom, has provided asylum for numberless groups of refugees. But the bulk of the population in the occupied territory has usually taken up the attitude that, with the defeat of their armed forces and the capitulation of their government, there was nothing much the conquered people could do about the situation.

A change has taken place in this attitude.

The problem of occupying a country now includes a new factor of growing importance which is that many of the so-called civilian population may not be disposed to accept the defeat of their armed forces as the end of the struggle. In a lecture to service officers I remarked: "This audience has been taught that, when carrying out military operations in the

Middle East, it is necessary to be careful to respect the special position of Moslem women and not to go into mosques with your shoes on! But who has ever been taught what to do in a situation when a Moslem woman lobs a bomb at you from the roof of a mosque?"

The growth of significance of non-official-military and passive resistance is due to several causes, viz: The technique of the use of arms has become widespread owing to training received by millions of men in two world wars; the development of small-sized bombs and automatic weapons has greatly facilitated terrorist activities; the masses have become more politically educated and apprised of what seems to them to be the importance of *ideas* such as nationalism.

This last-mentioned development is the most significant because it is an ideological force. All over the world the common man, whatever kind of government he endures, has become more politically conscious during the first half of this century. In particular the emotion of nationalism has become one of the most potent forces in the world and the cause of much tension. As mentioned earlier, the Communists have always understood the importance of this development and work hard to equate nationalism with Communism. The growth of nationalistic feelings amongst the masses is one of the reasons for the general tendency of war to become more and more ideological in its purpose.

The Soviet leaders were quick to exploit Russian nationalism in World War II and called it "the patriotic war" and during the war years various Russian national heroes of the Tsarist régime were dragged out of the dustbin and temporarily restored to their pedestals.

At the present time nationalism is probably the most potent force in the Arab world and our American allies sometimes find it hard to believe that neither dollars nor parades of force can anaesthetize nor defeat it.

However, this conception that the struggle is not to be regarded as at an end if the armed forces of the state are defeated is in an early stage of its evolution and has not yet become an officially recognized part of national defence policies. Therefore no thought has been given to the problem of what sort of resistance to occupation should be planned.

Should it be violent or passive, or a combination of the two? And how should the nation be trained for the selected method?

The phenomenon discussed above is important from the point of view of the subject of this book because its existence indicates that national groups are becoming psychologically attuned to the notion that a war is not ended when the armed forces lay down their arms. The masses do not yet realize that in modern war if the armed forces have been defeated the chances of a successful continuation of the struggle by *violent* civil resistance against an organized military force are slight. But the important development is the awareness of the people that the struggle is still in being and in due course it will become more widely understood that, with the defeat of the armed forces, violent methods have been exhausted and the new battle must be conducted non-violently.

There is not much of value for the purposes of this study to be learnt from the German occupation of Western Europe. We are considering a situation in which an occupation of the United Kingdom (and/or the E.T.O. nations if E.T.O. were formed) would be regarded as a continuation of the war and even—as we shall see—a state of affairs providing in the psychological sphere an intensification of the war. But the Nazi occupation of Europe was the sequel to a military victory *not* the prelude to a psychological struggle and the peoples of the occupied countries were still thinking of the war in military terms since they based their hopes on a liberation by allied armies. This is the important difference between what I conceive to be the background of an unopposed or only tokenly-opposed occupation and that of the European occupations of 1940-45.

From a general survey of what happened during World War II in a number of countries it seems that three parallel developments can be traced. First, each occupied territory had a government in London claiming to be the authority in exile. These governments, recognized by the British Government, collaborated with the British in organizing sabotage, intelligence work and guerrilla warfare resistance of various kinds in the occupied territories. The object of these activities was initially to make administration as difficult as possible for the

German authorities, and later on, as the plans for the invasion of the Continent matured, to help it forward by the provision of intelligence and sabotage of enemy communications.

Another of the developments was the behaviour and attitudes of the average man. I shall return to this in a moment.

Finally there was the third development, found to a greater or less extent in each occupied territory, that of the collaborators or Quislings.

The first phenomenon, that of underground anti-German active resistance, encouraged some people by making them feel that the spirit of national resistance was not dead; but on the other hand—as I discovered when soon after the war I travelled slowly through France looking into this matter—there were many people who did not approve of *La Résistance*, partly because they thought it useless if not harmful to the national interest and partly because a considerable number of criminals and bandits promptly joined up with the movement.

Near Briançon in the home territory of the Chasseurs Alpins regiment, I was told that some partisans had ambushed a small German convoy killing two Germans. As a result the Germans went to the nearest village and shot a number of men as reprisals. My informant asked me what good this attack on the convoy had done and assured me that the countryside had been anxious to see the partisans subdued. I heard similar stories in Belgium, where a whole village had been destroyed as a reprisal.

Although the violent resistance movement in the occupied territories provided many examples of extreme heroism and towards the end of the war were valuable as sources of intelligence, neither the German administrative authorities nor the German General Staff regarded them as being much more than a nuisance during the occupation. An exception to this existed in Russia, where the immensely long lines of communication of the German armies offered great scope to guerrilla warfare activities behind the fighting line and, as I know from first-hand information, the German Army which surrendered at Stalingrad had the greatest difficulty in keeping open its supply communications with Germany. But this was not the same as the case we are considering, because a war of movement was in progress, whereas in Western Europe it had come to an end with the capitulation or flight of the Government.

Furthermore the violent form of resistance we are considering is a reflection of a moral resistance, it is not a military campaign to expel the invaders by force. The active resisters who carry on the struggle by violence after the regular forces have capitulated are dependent for their existence on the collaboration in various degrees of intensity of thousands of non-terrorists. For example, the Mau Mau rebellion was only brought under control when large numbers of the Kikuyu tribe who were anti-Mau Mau were allowed to co-operate in the struggle and the toll of over 10,000 loyal Kikuyu dead shows that the Mau Mau leaders realized who were their most dangerous enemies. E.O.K.A. in Cyprus would not have lasted a month had it not received widespread support partly through fear, partly through sympathy, from the mass of the Cypriots.

Another aspect of the resistance movements question is this: their object is to create a political situation favourable to the occupied country.

A violent resistance movement goes into action, undertakes sabotage, shoots up prominent enemy individuals and generally creates what the occupying power would call a terrorist movement. The occupying power retaliates with collective punishments, executions, curfews and counter-terrorism. A situation may then build up in which the government of the occupying power finds itself under pressure from public opinion either at home or abroad or both. British Governments in my lifetime have had this experience in the cases of Palestine, Eire and India, and to a lesser extent in Cyprus. The French Government experienced this technique in Algeria.

World public opinion as echoed at the United Nations is becoming of significance, and in a democracy what the opposition thinks may be of decisive importance.

But the value to the occupied nation of the psychological effect on public opinion outside the occupied territories such as the creation of martyrs in the cause of liberty, etc., depends upon the political character of the occupying country. Hitler was quite indifferent to the reactions of world opinion to his anti-semitic policies and barbarities, and Communist governments show a like indifference when it is tactically expedient to do so. British Governments on the other hand have always been sensitive to terrorist or even political pressure from people under their control.

I come now to the second development in the occupied countries, the attitude of the average citizen to the German occupation. It is impossible to do more than generalize about this aspect of the subject. It would be of great value if a large-scale and scientifically organized enquiry were made into what thousands of ordinary people thought should be their behaviour *vis à vis* an occupying power. The result of enquiries made from a limited number of individuals in the Nazi-occupied territories is summarized below.

I. The average citizen had faith in varying degrees that he would be liberated. This hope, at a very low ebb in 1940, increased as the war proceeded.

II. In these circumstances there was a feeling that the right thing to do was to make the best of a bad business, carry on with one's daily life and await liberation.

III. There was no prepared policy or plan in any occupied country giving the citizens any guidance as to what their behaviour should be if the country were occupied.

IV. The mass of the people in the occupied territories who were not either active resisters or open collaborators seem to have varied in their attitude between that of "keeping ourselves to ourselves and having as little to do as possible with the enemy" and "life has to go on and business is business even if the customer is an enemy".

V. I can find little evidence that any attempts of significance were made either to organize any form of non-violent resistance or any form of political warfare against the occupying forces.

A partial exception to the above generalization is provided by the story of events in Norway where, after the defeat of the Norwegian forces, the resistance was of two kinds. From 1940-43 it was principally non-violent, but from 1943 to 1945 there was the growth of violent resistance organized from Britain and carried out by units parachuted into the country.

The first phase is of most interest from the point of view of this study.

When the Nazis invaded Norway they expected that so

genuine an Aryan and Nordic race would welcome them and their doctrines and at the end of the military campaign the Germans issued instructions to the occupying troops to be careful not to antagonize the people, and all administration was left in the hands of Norwegians. It was only in their attitude to the Storting that the invaders were tough, but the majority of Members of Parliament refused to function and after abortive negotiations the Germans issued decrees on 25th September, 1940 which turned Norway into what was virtually a German province administered by pro-German Councillors of State under the control of a Reichskommisar (Terboven) and backed by the Hird, a kind of Norwegian version of the German S.S.

Sustained efforts were then made to secure support of the judicial system, but the Supreme Court resigned in a body. Students' Unions were dissolved and replaced by Nazi unions. They were boycotted and collapsed. The Bishops refused to obey attempts to use the Church as an instrument of government and pastoral letters containing the correspondence between the Minister of Church Affairs and all Bishops were read in all churches.

In the winter of 1940 41 decrees were issued making it compulsory to display Quisling's portrait in schools, to eliminate the teaching of English and to teach history on Nazi lines. A nation-wide strike of teachers backed by parents and the Church was successful. Doctors and actors were two other professions which managed to defeat the Quisling Government.

By October 1941 the pro-German Government decided to adopt more violent methods and in March 1942 a great struggle began with the teachers, of whom 12,000 out of 14,000 refused to join a government-organized Teachers' Confederation. They were supported by the parents. 1,300 teachers were arrested and the schools were closed. By August 1942 the Government had to retreat and the schools re-opened. In April 1942 93 per cent of the clergy "disestablished" themselves from the state church and declared they were only in spiritual relation with the people.

A. K. Jameson, the author of *New Way in Norway*, a *Peace News* pamphlet on this subject, writes:

"If the question is asked whether the Norwegian experience goes to prove that the technique of non-violence offers an

efficient substitute for violence and can be successful in producing the desired results, the answer would appear to be that
it does and can in the moral and ideological realm. That is to
say, the occupying authorities completely failed to impose their
new order on Church, education, professional and sporting
organizations. These organizations were, with their funds and
buildings, taken over by the authorities and handed to the 2
per cent of the population who collaborated with them; but it
was only the material shell which was handed over. As regards
the spirit, that was kept untouched and untouchable and to the
end Church and schools continued to preach and teach on the
same lines as before the occupation. It was a magnificent
demonstration of faithfulness to an ideal and of staunchness in
face of physical suffering carried out over a period of years
during which the occupying authorities seemed to be all-
powerful and almost unchallenged in their career of conquest.
The moral and physical strain must have been intense and the
steadfastness displayed is worthy of the highest praise."

*   *   *

The conclusion I have reached after studying the Norwegian
story is that for many reasons the non-violent resistance
movement was operating in favourable circumstances which
would not often be repeated. What the Norwegian experience
indicates is that if the favourable circumstances are ignored and
replaced by a prolonged and careful training of the nation in
the tactics of non-violent resistance, very powerful and indestructible moral forces can be mobilized against an occupying
power.

Finally there was the third development, the collaborators or
Quislings. Now that war emotions have subsided it is possible
to take a more objective view of this subject than was possible
at a time when it was normal to regard all collaborators as
double-dyed traitors.

It is certain that amongst collaborators were men and women
whose principal motive was one of self-advancement or protection. They were the Vicars of Bray. But it would be a gross oversimplification to lump into this category every Western
European in an occupied territory who co-operated in any
way with the occupying forces.

A French friend of mine had a factory which made aircraft propellers. The Germans ordered him to keep in production and manufacture to their specification. He has said to me: "Should I have said 'To hell'' and been shot? The factory would have remained in production. And what about my work-people? It is true I was an armaments factory, but the principle would have been the same had I been making boots and been ordered to supply them to the German troops."

"What did you do?" I asked.

"I quickly tore up your News-Letters," he replied, "and then made a plan to keep production as slow as possible. The Germans became very suspicious; I managed to deceive them. I sent my chief engineer to the Messerschmidt factory in Germany with the excuse that we needed more know-how. I told him to stay as long as he could and spin out matters. As a result of all this, when France was liberated, I and my chief engineer were arrested and damn nearly shot as collaborators. It was impossible for me to produce documentary proof that some of my actions, apparently of a most collaborating character, had the secret purpose of hindering the German war effort."

To come to simpler cases:

Were a postman, an engine driver, an electrician at a power station, a dairyman, a policeman, a butcher, a newspaper reporter, Uncle Tom Cobley and all who carried on their jobs in Brussels, Amsterdam, Oslo, Copenhagen, Paris or in the villages COLLABORATORS? What about this case, known to me: Mlle. X in a French village near Amiens became the mistress of the German Major whose reservist troops occupied this area for two years until, to the distress of themselves and the locals, they were ordered to the Russian front. Visiting the village in 1945 I was astonished to see Mlle. X living a normal life and apparently having no trouble. The village barber explained to me that she had rendered a most useful service to the people, for the Major invariably followed her advice in all questions affecting the welfare of the villagers. If troops had to be billeted, Mlle. X knew which families could take them with the least hardship. The same barber informed me that when it was heard that the S.S. troops might pay a visit to the area, the local French and the German reservists connived against the

S.S. How does Mlle. X stand up to the charge of collaboration?

The conclusion I draw from these episodes, reflections and estimations is that in general no plans had been made at the national level in the West European countries, or probably at any other level, as to what should be the correct course of action of a citizen in the event of the national territory being occupied. It was assumed that the national armed forces would prevent the occupation taking place.

Perhaps it is too much to expect that plans should have been made, because plans must be related to a purpose and all defence thinking in 1939 and before was geared to the notion that the only way to win or lose "a war" was by the actions of military force, a delusion—as I have pointed out in Chapter I —which was the child of a misunderstanding about the real nature of War (*werre*).

But if, as I argue in this book, there is another and perhaps a better way of winning a war or even preventing a war from degenerating into violence than the use or threat to use force, then plans can and must be made well in advance to deal with all contingencies of which a possible occupation by the enemy is certainly one of the most serious.

It seems to me obvious that a defence system of non-violence against violence must be as carefully planned, both tactically and strategically, as an attack which will be carried out by trained men, fortified by military tradition and directed by a highly intelligent general staff. The fact that the whole conception of defence (and attack) by non-violent methods is strange to most people makes long and thorough training and planning essential.

What those plans might be and how the nation should be trained to implement them will be discussed in the next two chapters.

CHAPTER THIRTEEN

RESISTANCE WHEN OCCUPIED

IN WAR THE WILL to win is the first essential. In a war to defend our way of life our object must be, if Great Britain is subjected to an enemy occupation, not only to retain the essentials of our way of life, but to do so in such a manner that we change the enemy's mind and either convince him that he should leave us alone to pursue our way of life or, better still, convince him that our way of life and our ideas are superior to those he holds and which he wishes to force upon us.

Therefore in the struggle between democracy and Communism the first step in preparing the nation for an occupation and how to deal with it, is to instil the conviction into our people that an enemy occupation is only an episode, a battle in a campaign, a continuation of the struggle in a new form and not an event which must be regarded as a hopeless disaster only to be retrieved by a forceful liberation from outside (likely in any future war to be nuclear in character) or negotiations involving loss of territory, indemnities, reparation and other material concessions.

I go further and say that notwithstanding the miseries, hardships and deaths likely to be associated with an occupation, the event should be regarded as providing means whereby the enemy is inevitably brought into close contact with a way of life which he wishes to destroy, but which we believe has inherent advantages over his. It was interesting to notice that according to the U.N. report on events in Hungary, the Russian authorities could not rely on troops which had been stationed in Hungary and had to use Asiatic troops who believed that they were fighting French and British imperialists in connection with Suez! It is certainly a fact that the rulers of the Soviet Union take a good deal of trouble to prevent any number of their citizens making informal and personal contacts with the free way of life.

In military operations it is an ordinary occurrence for

territory to be deliberately abandoned to the enemy as a strategical measure in order to lure him into a disadvantageous tactical situation. Anyone who has had experience of operations in mountain country knows the dangers of the easy advance down the valley unless the peaks on either side are simultaneously occupied.

If therefore I write that an enemy occupation of Great Britain by a power energized by a totalitarian way of life can be regarded as a strategical opportunity to engage the enemy more closely in the psychological battle, as well as a tactical defeat in the military battle, I trust I shall not be told that I am advocating that we should at all costs seek to bring about an occupation. This would be asking rather too much—at any rate in 1957.

*   *   *

The answers to the problems of how a people and especially the people of the United Kingdom shall carry on the struggle when their homeland is occupied by the enemy has never been worked out in advance by the best minds of the country as a deliberate part of the defence plans of the nation. The most an individual can hope to do in tackling this novel and complex question is to suggest ideas which may be thought worthy of further discussion.

To be effective this resistance must be organized in advance and not expected to spring out of the occupation in an *ad hoc* manner, any more than armed forces are expected to be created when military operations begin. A soldier of sorts can be trained in three months; to train a fairly competent non-violent resister might require three years.

I shall return to the question of planning resistance.

The second principle is concerned with the strategy and tactics of the resistance because, until this is determined, planning and preparations cannot take place.

Resistance under an occupation can be of three kinds:

> Violent
> Non-Violent
> Combining violent and non-violent

Which of these three methods should be the foundation of our defence?

The reasons which lead me to suggest it should be non-violent are as follows:

1. A violent resistance, i.e. sabotage, terrorism, etc., is only a continuation of organized military resistance or an attempt to create military resistance where no military forces exist and it has been argued in these pages that nuclear energy in war has created a situation calling for a revision of our ideas about the use of violence in defence.

2. Our object is to defend our way of life. It is evident that the institutions (see Chapter III) which are the framework of our way of life cannot continue to function in their normal form during an occupation. We are therefore left *with the idea or spirit of our way of life* which is what we have to defend.

Writing on this subject in the *Eastern Economist* on 30th August, 1957, "Odysseus" observes:

"Civil resistance with violence must seriously affect the social fabric of the nation adopting it. Organized fighting in armies is disciplined . . . the practice of violence in, as it were, an orderly and responsible manner by bodies of men subject to discipline does not undermine the Rule of Law and social fabric of the nation as partisans practising guerrilla warfare do . . . in France after World War II as many as probably 100,000 'traitors' were executed in the name of justice. Most of these cases were in fact private vendettas or acts of irresponsible haste carried out by the rival parties of the French resistance."

The same author points out that "Gandhiji insisted at first that mass civil disobedience should not be initiated until a 'non-violent' atmosphere had been created" but that he yielded to pressure and agreed to give it a trial, but called off civil disobedience in February 1921 after excesses by a mob.

The author whom I am quoting (it is fair to state) was writing against the idea that non-violent resistance was possible in Britain "where only a decimal fraction are attuned to pacifism, of whom the majority are ordinary flesh and blood".

3. A plan whereby the people of the United Kingdom substituted a national scheme of violent "civil" resistance for

G

conventional military resistance would have no moral effect either on world public opinion or that of the enemy, and the efficacy of the defence depends upon the extent to which it can generate this moral force.

In February 1957 I was in Johannesburg during the extraordinary boycott of the bus services by Africans. The impressive and, to many non-Africans, alarming feature of this affair was its non-violence. To stand at the outskirts of an African township and witness thousands of Africans who were walking 15 miles a day to and from work as a matter of principle and to see this black tide of humanity move past over a hundred police as if the latter were non-existent created an eerie feeling. Not a look at the police; not a gesture of defiance or word of abuse and everyone knew that the police were ready at the slightest provocation to go for the crowd. But the police stood there baffled and in a curious way were publicly humiliated. It was the astonishing and patient self-discipline of the boycotters which impressed many observers with a sense of the tremendous force of the African resistance to racial policies.

A highly educated African leader said to me: "If our people will remain non-violent, and we must trust the authorities to back this state of affairs by retaining all the arms, we are bound to win. We have only to sit still for a week and the Government will sue for peace."

An accurate and detailed historical study of conflicts between groups in which non-violent resistance played an important part does not seem to exist.

Non-violent resistance in various forms was conspicuous in the Hungarian struggle against Austrian rule from 1850-67 led by the great patriot Deak whose policy was entirely along non-violent lines.

From 1919-22 in Egypt during the struggle for Egyptian independence there was a non-violent aspect of Egyptian policy particularly the successful boycott of the Milner mission. In India there was Ghandi's policy of non-violence and the German passive resistance against the French occupation of the Ruhr from January to September 1923. A study of such movements would also include some account of non-co-operative policies by Sinn Fein in the Irish struggle, in the course of which it was said: "We have two governments in Ireland and neither can protect us from the other."

In the Ruhr episode the German government: (a) Prohibited all German citizens from rendering any assistance to the invaders: (b) Guaranteed financial compensation to any German who lost his means of livelihood. German officials acted as if the invaders were non-existent; post offices, telephone exchanges, newspapers and establishments of all kinds refused to have any dealings with "the enemy". The French retaliated by expelling 150,000 Germans from the Ruhr, cutting off the area from the Reich, seizing public buildings and private property. The French were obliged to take over the coal mines and had to import 12,000 railwaymen to keep communications in operation. The occupation of the Ruhr resulted in a Pyrrhic victory for the French They ruined German credit and made it still more impossible for her to pay reparations. There was also a violent side to the Ruhr episode and several hundred fatal casualties on both sides. Violence also occurred in parallel, as it were, with the non-violent policies, in the Hungarian, Egyptian, Irish and Indian struggles and the same duality of policy was to be observed in the Palestine conflict between the Israelis and the British mandatory power.

It is interesting to note that men like Deak (in Hungary), Redmond (in Ireland), Dr. Weizman (in Palestine), Ghandi (in India), the outstanding leaders were always against violence.

A study of the evidence available leads me to the following conclusions:

(a) That the non-violent side of all these struggles invariably presented "the enemy" with the most difficult and perplexing problems.

(b) That the effectiveness of the non-violent activities were always reduced by violence.

(c) That the value of violence depended upon the political climate inside "the enemy country".

(d) That all the cases of which we have records were combinations of violence and non-violence and (with the exception of certain racial episodes where no arms were available to the resisters) we have no evidence about a completely non-violent struggle.

(e) That non-violence is much more difficult than violence because it involves a psychological change amongst the resisters towards the enemy. The non-violent resistance ethic can be summed up as defeating the enemy by an internal change on the part of the resister in which "hatred" of the enemy becomes "love and compassion".

This involves controlling the emotions of what Odysseus (see page 193) described as "ordinary flesh and blood".

II

If non-violent resistance and non-violent attack is to be the basis of the strategy of defence, how could this idea be given tactical content? To answer this question we must assume that the nation has accepted and understands the principles of the policy. To the best of my belief there has been very little research on this subject of tactics which is not surprising because a first requirement for research would be accurate information about past experiences which, as mentioned earlier, does not amount to much.

However, even if we knew much more than we do about the previous non-violent resistance movements, I think it unlikely we would discover from these experiences the rules and practices appropriate to the policy in the nuclear age.

There is an important difference between the non-violent resistance movements of the past and the conception which is being discussed in this book. In the past non-violent resistance has always been an adjunct to violence of some kind or perhaps a movement *faute de mieux* because the facilities for violence were not available. Non-violent movements in the past often bore the same kind of relationship to violence as political warfare has hitherto borne to military operations. But in this book we are examining the potentialities of non-violence as the governing policy and one to which as much attention would be paid and forethought given as is regarded normal for military defence plans. In 1942 the American pacifists produced some plans which presupposed:

"A voluntarily disarmed country, an unprovoked invasion of

this country (the U.S.A.) by a foreign power and a government and people who have decided to resist this invasion by non-violent methods".[1] In this pamphlet the author lays down the following four principles of unarmed defence:

1. No service or supplies to be furnished to the invaders.
2. No orders to be obeyed except those of the constitutional civil authorities.
3. No insult or injury to be offered to the invader.
4. All public officials to be pledged to die rather than surrender.

An attempt is then made to translate these principles into an outline of practice.

The following extracts indicate the nature of the author's proposals:

"Meeting with no opposition other than ordinary traffic regulations, the enemy commander . . . enters the City Hall and is received with courtesy by the Mayor . . . who refuses the order to surrender and is taken prisoner. The first Vice-Mayor automatically succeeds, but the invaders exclude him from the City Hall, setting in his place a traitor or officer of their own. Executives and clerks continue to perform their duties until commands arrive from the enemy usurper, when they either ignore the orders or cease work altogether, quietly destroying combinations and documents if opportunity affords. The City departments of fire and the police with the public utility services of telegraph, telephone and electricity, continue to function under their regular heads until these receive enemy orders. At this point they, too, will disregard specific commands or declare an instantaneous strike. Workers in garages, gas stations, airports and railroads will go on serving the civil population until interfered with and resume work if and when pressure is removed. . . ."

The writer faces up to the hypothesis of:

". . . an implacable commander under an unscrupulous government, supported by a political party quite reckless of

[1] *Pacifism and Invasion* by J. W. Hugham.

world or minority opinion" so that "an actual battle is under way, between starvation and enemy violence on the one hand and the will of a selected civilian population on the other."

In general the plan proposed for a non-violent resistance policy in the U.S.A. is that of the scorched earth policy and a kind of sit-down strike on a national scale.

I do not find this idea convincing for several reasons. In the first place it is out of the question to suppose that a nation will go, as it were, on hunger strike to the point of death in order to put the invaders in an embarrassing position *vis-à-vis* world public opinion, or their domestic public opinion if it has any significance.

To mention but one example illustrating the impracticability of this kind of non-violent resistance, no mother will deliberately allow her child to die of starvation for the sake of defending the free way of life. Nor is it necessary or logical that this contingency should occur; in order to defend the free way of life it is neither necessary nor desirable to invite the nation to make a mass exodus from life. We can leave that to nuclear warfare.

A sit-down strike on the part of the nation—if it could be organized—presupposes two conditions: first that the invaders can be made to feel a moral responsibility for maintaining the life of the nation and feel it so strongly that they acquiesce in any conditions the people of the occupied nation demand as the price of continuing to operate the economy. Secondly, and this is a weightier argument, that the occupiers have a manifest self-interest in the maintenance of the life of the nation.

In any circumstance reasonably probable, an occupier would have an interest of a purely selfish character in seeing that the economic life of the occupied nation continued to function in certain respects. I can imagine no circumstance in which an army of occupation *would wish* to be surrounded by millions of desperate and starving civilians.

But the main objections to proposals of the kind made in the American pamphlet is that they are negative in principle. Their object is solely that of making the occupation difficult for the enemy. This is desirable, but it is not the whole story. The object of non-violent resistance must be to *make the occupation dangerous for the enemy*. It cannot be "dangerous" to him from a military point of view, it must therefore be made dangerous to him from a political warfare angle, for this is the battlefield on which, if victory can be achieved, it will be total.

To put it quite simply, the question is this: "Is it conceivable that as a result of an occupation of the U.K. (and/or Western Europe) by the Soviet Union, Communism would be defeated and overcome by democratic ideas?"

It is conceivable, because anything which is thinkable is possible, but the practical question is how to plan it? One can also imagine a state of affairs in which the leaders of the Soviet Union, contemplating the preparations which had been made in the West to deal psychologically with an occupation might (since Communists are exceptionally well aware of the power of ideas) recoil from its danger.

This would reproduce the idea of the deterrent in another form. To the critic who says: "Are you seriously suggesting that Mr. Khrushchev (or whoever is at any moment in charge in the Soviet Union) would be deterred from an occupation policy by fear of the consequences to Communism?" My reply is: "I am, provided we can so organize ourselves that it is a dangerous psychological adventure for the Soviet Union to occupy the West and as I believe this can be achieved (or at the least the matter should be thoroughly investigated) I have more faith in this psychological deterrent that in the present H-Bomb retaliation deterrent."

The first principle of non-violent resistance in the conditions we are discussing is that it must be psychological. The whole struggle must be kept within the field of ideas. Therefore I rule out any terrorism, sabotage and violence. Terrorism would not baffle the enemy but be welcomed by him as something concrete, easily recognized and a legitimate excuse for violent and bloody reprisals. I have pointed out in Chapter III that the basic root of our way of life is located in the individual and we must therefore start by considering the proper course for the individual and later on see how individual actions can be co-ordinated.

A guide to individual conduct during an occupation (except in general terms) by the Soviet Union is as impossible to formulate as it is to particularize how an individual should be a Christian; an infinite variety of circumstances call for as many specific actions.

But general rules suggested as a guide to conduct for the individual are outlined below.

1. The economic life of the country to be maintained, that is to say, transport services, industrial production, agriculture, distribution and all activities concerned with the body-keeping business of the nation should proceed so far as possible in a normal manner or in accordance with directions issued by the occupying power.

2. As regards government, the attitude towards the enemy should be: "We have our well-established administrative arrangements and if you do not like them we await to hear from you what alternative you have in mind."

3. To refuse *at all costs* to say or write anything contrary to the principles of our way of life or to accept denial of freedom of speech and association.

4. To use every opportunity in personal contact with the occupying forces to expose the falacies of Communism and advantages of democracy.

5. In general to behave *vis-à-vis* the occupying forces with dignity and moral superiority. This is the key rule.

To many people these suggestions will seem unrealistic. I can imagine a Berliner who went through the horrors of the Russian occupation of that city rubbing his eyes with amazement at the fifth suggestion and regarding it as fantastic nonsense.

But it must be remembered that the occupation of Berlin was the climax of a battle and I am considering the circumstance of an occupation which has *not* been resisted by military force and of a nation trained (see Chapter XIV) to deal with this hypothesis. The distinction between an occupation as the climax of a military battle and one as the beginning of a psychological struggle is of the utmost importance. It is the difference between the argument of force and the force of an argument.

If it is to be assumed that in the event of an unresisted Russian occupation, which might begin with the arrival of a Russian airborne division at London Airport, all the personnel of this division would emerge from their planes and, without further ado, proceed to massacre the inhabitants of the neighbouring suburbs, then I must agree that there is not much more to be said. But I see no reason why this assumption should be valid and many reasons against it. I do not regard it as reasonable to suppose that the rulers of the Soviet Union would desire to occupy the United Kingdom for the sole purpose of destroying the population. Unless we are to make the further unreal assumption that Russians *qua* Russians are uniquely desirous of personally killing people, preferably helpless women and children; the elimination of the British population would be more simply and speedily accomplished by the use of H-Bombs.

The reader who finds it hard to take seriously ideas such as those in the five suggestions should ask himself whether he has succeeded in dismissing from his mind the notion that resistance must be violent to be effective that, if regular military operations end in defeat, the only hope is guerrilla warfare and that if this is not practicable or is suppressed, all is lost? And, equally important, has he been able to suppose that far from "all being lost" an opportunity exists in the case of an occupation for an offensive in the psychological field?

If he cannot at least *think* in such terms (the necessary preliminary to action) then he is not yet through the thought barrier!

Let us now look at the five suggestions in greater detail. They fall into two groups: The first two are concerned with material aspects of the life of the nation, the last three with ideas and attitudes of mind. There is some World War II experience of the first two suggestions, both in a positive and a negative form. In France, Norway and the Low Countries, after organized military resistance had ceased, life went on. There were rationing, military requisition, forced labour and other grave inconveniences. Sometimes worse, sometimes not so bad as the inconveniences voluntarily imposed by the democratic peoples on themselves. Even in Nazi Germany the extent to which women participated in the war effort was less than that in Britain. Once the tide of military operations had receded, the shops did business, the peasants tilled their fields, the railways operated, the letters (sometimes censored) were delivered, the newspapers circulated.

It was to the interest of both the occupiers and the occupied that this should be so and it is hard to imagine circumstances in which this would not be the case. An exception might be provided by a case in which the enemy required the land for surplus population, but that argument does not apply to a struggle between the Soviet Union and the United Kingdom.

If one of the purposes of an occupation of Britain by the Soviet Union would be to milk British industry for the benefit of Soviet consumers—as the Soviet Union milked the satellite states for a period until Moscow realized that to overdo this was self-defeating—then the Russians would have to take steps to see that imports or raw materials were somehow maintained. Except for coal the indigenous products of the United Kingdom are of no significance and a demand by the Russians for large deliveries of coal would simply mean that the production of British industry would decline and it is obvious that a Russia determined to milk Britain would prefer capital goods and consumer goods to raw materials. One can imagine a Soviet Government demanding ships, cars, diesel locomotives, machine tools but, to ensure delivery of the goods, workers and machines must be supplied with food and raw materials.

That the Soviet leaders are—as one would expect—realists in such matters was brought to my notice in 1945 at a state banquet in Moscow where my neighbour was M. Maisky, sometime Soviet Ambassador in London. In 1945 he was in charge of German prisoner of war camps and he told me that their labour output had been unsatisfactory and various "measures" had been taken to remedy this state of affairs. I remarked that these "measures" were presumably not very pleasant. He replied that the "measures" had raised difficulties and went on to explain that in order to get more work out of the Germans they had been given incentives in the form of cigarettes and more food and the difficulties arose from the circumstance that the prisoners were getting more than the local inhabitants, who had protested.

What is almost totally lacking is any experience relating to the second group of suggestions, which deal with moral resistance in its relation to the moral offensive.

In most forms of non-violent resistance of which there are records the object of the occupied people seems to have been chiefly directed towards making the occupation so difficult and inconvenient for the occupiers that they would feel the occupied were being unjustly treated.

In the case of the Irish independence movement there was, of course, the long political struggle at Westminster independent of the active violence of Sinn Fein.

In the hypothetical case we are considering, i.e. a Soviet occupation of Britain, the circumstances would be different from those in Ireland, Palestine, Egypt (at various times) and India, where the issue was not a difference of fundamental ideas, but a difference as to whether the granting of independence to these countries at a certain time (or the interpretation of the mandate in the case of Palestine) was or was not the proper course of democratic action. The Democracy versus Communism clash is of a different order of psychological conflict, it is a conflict of principles. A closer parallel is to be found in the racial question in the Union of S. Africa, or the Negro question in the Southern States of the U.S.A.

We must therefore consider the practical application of suggestions 3, 4 and 5 in terms of principles.

It may help if we select an institution such as the B.B.C. and consider the duty of a member of the staff during an occupation. I assume the Soviet administration would appoint a controller in general charge of policy. I conceive it to be the duty of the Corporation's employees to co-operate in the transmission of straight news and announcements and entertainment, music, etc., but to refuse to co-operate in the transmission of programmes designed to promote Communism. The senior British official allowed to function should make it his business to wage a psychological battle with the Russian controller and be prepared to be liquidated rather than surrender on principles in the knowledge that his successor would continue the battle, down to the most junior member of the staff. Entertainers and broadcasters would continue to function, taking every opportunity by ridicule, inuendo and even tone of voice to denigrate everything to do with the principles and practices of the enemy and to contrast it unfavourably with our way of life. Ridicule is a most potent weapon.

The same technique would be used by the Press. The object of a skilful editor under a Communist occupation should not be (*a*) to close down the paper or (*b*) to be so truculent that the enemy closes it down. His purpose should be to cause differences of opinion in the enemy administration as to whether or not his paper should be closed down. For it is certain that in a complex community the continuation of a Press is as essential to the occupier as it is to the occupied and a situation in which a Communist administration is obliged to close down the whole Press is a victory for the opposition. But better still if the Press can remain alive and be a kind of secret and subtle weapon against the occupier. If during an occupation the B.B.C. and Press were so skilfully handled that in sheer exasperation the Soviet administration closed them down completely then—so far as these two institutions were concerned—the struggle would move into the second phase in which illegal and clandestine news-sheets and bulletins and radio transmissions might come into operation.

Writers and all those persons in the nation who can be broadly described as the intellectuals or intelligentsia would be expected to recognize their special and dangerous duties as leaders in the struggle. They would be expected to put into practice the saying that "the pen is mightier than the sword". Martyrdom might be the fate of many of these leaders.

I have mentioned earlier that whilst the basis of psychological resistance to, and attack on the whole moral position of, the occupier must be the *conduct of the individual whose duty it is to remember that whilst there is breath in his body he must never give in mentally or abandon his right to be a free man, but proclaim his principles and practise them wherever and whenever it is possible to do so*, yet there is strength in unity. Our psychological defence and counter-attack, if ever the United Kingdom were occupied by the forces of a totalitarian power such as the Soviet Union, if it is to be as effective as possible, calls for long and careful preparation and a national organization.

Finally, no one is better aware than this author that the suggestions made in this chapter as to how the five principles should be applied only cover a very small part of the national life and are necessarily tentative in character. Nor have I attempted to consider how these practices would be linked up with similar policies in other E.T.O. countries. It will be remembered that it is proposed that one of the three sections of

E.T.O. at both the national and international levels should be concerned with the organizations of the Home Fronts both from the point of view of building up a stronger feeling of personal loyalty to democracy and its institutions and of training the nations to operate non-violent resistance during an occupation.

The two tasks are inseparable, but "home work" for democracy, or better education for citizenship, is an indispensable preliminary to the organizing of the nation for non-violent resistance. We can find an analogy in the military field where it has long been recognized that in the words of Napoleon the moral is to the physical as three is to one and that technical military training is far more effective if it is given to people who know and believe in the cause for which they are being trained to fight.

As will be seen in the next chapter, the training of the nation in the new policy of defence is not something which can be achieved in a short time and it is in the course of the implementation of this programme of defence training that the techniques of applying the principles, either those mentioned above or improvements on them, would emerge.

CHAPTER FOURTEEN

THE TRAINING OF THE NATION

A POLICY OF TRAINING the able-bodied people of a nation in defence techniques has been accepted as normal in most countries of Western Europe since the Napoleonic wars. In earlier days there was the feudal system, which included defence among the mutual obligations of its members. This was succeeded by the period of the whole-time professional fighter, either nationally-recruited or hired as a mercenary, and then Europe moved into the era of conscription.

It was mentioned in Chapter IX that for centuries the people of Great Britain had good reason to believe that, isolated by the waters of the Channel and protected by powerful fleets, they need not take into account in their defence arrangements the likelihood of a successful invasion.

This happy position began to deteriorate at the beginning of the twentieth century and a change of thought started on the subject of national service, which had been traditionally regarded as non-British notwithstanding the use of the press-gang in the Napoleonic wars.

During World War I there was a gradual extension of compulsory military service as it became clear that God seemed to be on the side of the big battalions[1] and the immense military effort needed could not be sustained by the methods and traditions of "the first hundred-thousand". The revolutionary departure from our three-hundred-year-old traditional strategy which took place when we decided to raise immense armies for use overseas and were thus committed to sustaining a strong navy and army *and* providing economic support for our allies, had profound consequences on our defence capacity; although these were not to be fully revealed until the people of Britain were called upon to shoulder the strain of World War II, which involved an effort to have a large fleet, a large army, make a

[1] He had not then let man into the secrets of nuclear energy.

stupendous arms production effort AND maintain a great air-force and civil defence organization. This achievement crippled the nation as severely as the effort of World War I crippled France so that she collapsed in 1940. In World War II, and indeed a few months before the outbreak of hostilities, the principle of compulsory military service for males was accepted by Parliament and the emergence of World War III (in cold form) in 1946 made it necessary to continue a policy which the British still hoped could be regarded as a temporary measure during hot wars.

At the moment of writing it is official policy to abolish National Service although it remains to be seen whether even our much-reduced military commitments will be satisfied through voluntary enlistment in the forces. Many authorities doubt that it will be possible. After the war, efforts were made to maintain the civil defence organizations, but although authorities such as Field Marshal Lord Montgomery have pointed out that the almost complete lack of adequate civil defence in the European homelands of Nato is a grave, if not almost fatal defect in our defences, the whole theory of civil defence has been severely shaken by the advent of nuclear weapons. The public admission of British Ministers that the civil population cannot be defended against this form of attack has not encouraged people to join Civil Defence in response to the argument that any defence is better than none and perhaps only conventional bombs would be used.

Reference was made on page 179 to some of the quaint ideas about civil defence which have emerged from Whitehall. Nevertheless I wish to say clearly that as things are it is wrong and unpatriotic to suggest that civil defence training is useless. Until it is replaced by the new kind of civil defence suggested in this book it should be supported. It is by far the most logical and sensible aspect of conventional war (and therefore the most neglected) and would certainly do some good—one may be uncertain about how much—in nuclear war.

The outline of events sketched in the preceding pages of this book entitle us to conclude that, albeit with reluctance, the British people have, during the past 50 years, come round to the view—long accepted as normal by Continental peoples—that some form of national training for defence is part, or may have to be accepted as part, of the duties of a citizen in a democratic state.

This duty, either in its military or civil form, is not in favour at the moment (1957) largely because the ordinary citizen has his doubts whether, even if we broke our backs endeavouring to maintain large conventional forces (which would mean two years' National Service), our defences would be much more adequate than they now are.

If, however, it could be shown to the satisfaction of reasonable people that *national training for a different kind of defence* is a worthwhile activity, they would not object to doing their duty, the more so if they could be convinced that in terms of time and effort and dislocation of civilian life the new training had immense advantages over the traditional form of National Service.

II

It would be necessary for the Government to declare that it intends to work out a policy for the purpose of training the nation to conduct war through non-violent activities and create the national framework within which the behaviour of the civil population (behaviour which was briefly considered in Chapter XII) in the event of an occupation would be co-ordinated and strengthened by co-operative action. In order to consider how such a policy could be implemented I must make the assumption that it is the will of the nation that it should be done.

In terms of practical politics we are to-day (1957) only in the opening phases of the great debate about the practicability and desirability of undertaking this second great revolution in our defence arrangements.

The first great revolution in our defence strategy took place in 1911 when we decided to abandon a strategy of defence which had served us well for three centuries and commit ourselves to raising and maintaining a large army for use in the main theatre of war. This was a very startling and far-reaching decision, the consequences of which are with us to-day. It can be argued that it was a mistake and that we should have stuck to the strategy, which defeated Louis XIV and Napoleon, of basing our military effort on sea-power and finance and using our small army for secondary campaigns. But the fact is that the United Kingdom was only able to exert military strength of the first order of magnitude when "naval force" had as its only rival other "naval force". The arrival of the aeroplane altered all that and as military strength became more and more a combination of air-sea-and-manpower Great Britain was bound to descend into the ranks of the second league, a movement down the scale of military power previously experienced first by the Spaniards, then the Dutch and later by the French.

Has the time come for the U.K. to undertake a second great revolution in defence strategy?

What follows is no more than an attempt to show what could be done if a positive decision were reached, as a result of the debate, that the second revolution should be launched.

The first thought is that the job would take a long time; perhaps twenty years must elapse before the nation, which is mentally anchored (by a cable of increasingly rusty doubt) to the traditional methods, would be attuned to the idea of defending its way of life by the new methods. The business would have to start in the schools of the country so as to create a generation convinced that training in civil defence meant training in the techniques of non-violent resistance and was part of the normal duties of a citizen. The teaching would apply to the youth of both sexes and the co-operation of the teaching profession would be essential. We should have to be careful not to impose doctrines on teachers, but in fact if the broad principle of N.V.R. were adopted, the teaching required would only be an extension and an increase of attention and effort on the teaching of what is called to-day civics or citizenship. There would be nothing politically controversial about the proposal for more educational emphasis on the true values of our way of life.

It must be emphasized that it would be useless to attempt to train a nation to defend itself, i.e. its way of life (even at the cost of sacrificing material considerations), by psychological methods unless a large proportion of the electorate were in an advanced state of educated citizenship and therefore understood what it was all about. Having had some experience of seeking the support of the British electorate at Parliamentary by-elections my guess is that about 10 per cent. of the electorate in the United Kingdom are at the required level of political development. The proportion is increasing and in the British electorate as a whole there is an immense capacity for sound solid common sense capable of judging the capacity of leaders and accepting or rejecting their ideas.

If a class in a secondary school to-day is discussing defence, Nato, the United Nations and so forth, an intelligent child is entitled to ask: "What are people supposed to do if this country were occupied by a totalitarian power?" I doubt whether the collective wisdom of the Cabinet could give him a considered reply other than the late Earl of Oxford's classic "Wait and see!"

But whilst the full implementation of the new policy on defence would have gradually to mature through the educational structure of the Kingdom, other measures would have to be started elsewhere.

For example institutions such as the Press, the B.B.C., the Banks and Insurance Companies, through their associations and in consultation with the Unions concerned, should be invited by the British section of E.T.O. to work out what instructions should be given to their staffs in the event of an occupation and what training would be required to enable those instructions to be effectively put into force.

The proposals now being discussed are not only related to the idea for a progressive change-over in our defence policy from violence to non-violence. They are also of practical significance in our present violent defence arrangements, unless we are to believe that we can either rule out an invasion and occupation as being unthinkable or that if it is not unthinkable it is to be accepted as the final defeat.

A government which has to admit that it has abandoned all hope of protecting the civil life of the nation (and in so doing they have been commendably honest) can hardly claim that an occupation is out of the question and to accept that this event must be the end of our national story is unworthy of our traditions. Although the facts would rightly be kept secret, I suppose that in the event of an invasion there must be some plans to deal with such questions as the location of the Cabinet, perhaps an embryonic scheme for regional controllers, the use of emergency ports, the decentralization of broadcasting and so forth. But if such plans do exist they are—if past experience is any guide—of a sketchy character and are only germane to the period of armed conflict. There is a vast difference between a plan, for example (which may exist), for the removal of Parliament from London whilst hostilities are proceeding, and a plan (which we can be sure does not exist) whereby Members of Parliament, if the country is effectively occupied, proceed to their constituencies to undertake leadership in the continuation of the national struggle in accordance with the five suggested principles mentioned in the previous chapter. It may be that the first act of an enemy occupier would be to seize, deport or execute all Members of Parliament. In that event there must be arrangements for other persons to take their places and others to take theirs.

The parliamentary constituency might both on psychological and practical grounds be the most appropriate geographical unit on which to build up local non-violent resistance centres.

The Communists who, through much thought and years of experience, know a great deal about the practice and theory of political warfare, start with the cell. There is much to be said in favour of the small group of dedicated persons. The only thing objectionable about the Communist cell is that it exists to propagate and support ideas deadly to democracy and does so by wicked actions. "Cells" can be composed of persons who belong to the small minority of a nation who are prepared to be exceptionally zealous in a cause. There is no reason to suppose that a democratic nation is incapable of producing such people who, during a long and arduous psychological struggle with the occupying forces, would be the hard core of the resistance and—at a risk to their lives—would give leadership and example to their weaker brethren.

It is just as noble to die under torture because one has been convicted of activities of a psychological nature in support of democracy and against totalitarianism as it is to be incinerated by an H-bomb if the deterrent does not deter. I reproduce overleaf a poem reprinted from a book called *A Mother Fights Hitler*.[1]

1 Allen and Unwin, 1940.

Thoughts are free,
Who can guess them?
They fly past
Like evening shadows.
No man can know them,
No hunter shoot them:
One thing is sure:
Thoughts are free.

I think what I will
And what rejoices me:
Yet all in silence
As is befitting.
My wish and my longing
Can none forbid:
One thing is sure:
Thoughts are free.

Though they shut me up
In a dungeon dark
All this is vain
Availing them nothing;
For then my thoughts
Shiver the bolts
And shatter the walls:
Thoughts are free!

The hero of the book is Hans Litten, son of the authoress who struggled in vain to save her son's life in the Nazi persecution in pre-war days. He was a brilliant young intellectual and recognized as highly dangerous by the Nazis. He fought them relentlessly at the psychological level in various concentration camps and when in one camp the prisoners were ordered to put up an entertainment, Hans Litten went on to the stage and, to an audience including many Nazis, recited this poem.

This is one small example of non-violent resistance and it was a world tragedy that the groups in Germany which in Dachau and elsewhere were fighting for democracy received no support from the democratic world, which could have been in the form of moral and economic pressure on Hitler.

I have mentioned the Press as being a key institution in the maintenance of the free way of life and suggested that certain tactics might be adopted. But preparations should also be made to deal with the possibility that the enemy, exasperated by the Fabian tactics of a Press subtly encouraging and supporting psychological resistance, would close down the public Press. There should be prepared plans in detail for an underground Press producing leaflets and news-letters with an underground distribution system.

The military authorities in Cyprus could provide some interesting information as to how this has been done by E.O.K.A.

This example of the Press has been chosen to illustrate the argument that all democratic institutions which are concerned with ideas should have plans ready worked out in detail in advance, and practised in the form of exercises, to deal with an occupation by a totalitarian enemy.

The training of the nation in the technique of non-violent resistance would be the over-all responsibility of the Minister representing Britain in E.T.O., the allied organization for the conduct of psychological defence at home and attack abroad. As the whole scheme developed this Minister would be the *de facto* minister of defence. Although it would take us too far afield to go into details it seems probable that the change in national defence policy now being considered would involve a reorganization of our Ministries and in particular a change in the status of the Foreign Office. In the past it has been the business of the defence services to be prepared to implement Clauzewitz's theory that war is a continuation of policy by other means. But in this nuclear age and in terms of the definition of War (*werre*) adopted in Chapter I we ought perhaps to think of: "policy being a continuation of war (or the conduct of war) by non-violent means." As things are to-day the defence policy of the deterrent governs foreign policy, and one is tempted to say *is* foreign policy.

It was suggested in Chapter X when we were discussing the need for an Allied Political Warfare organization that it would have three main tasks viz: home front opinion; uncommitted nations' opinion; enemy opinion. The measures we have been considering in this chapter belong to the home front section of the British part in E.T.O. or, if the conception of an allied organization does not materialize, the organization would be a British Ministry seeking such co-operation as was practical with other states concerned with the Communist menace.

The first task of the British ministry should be to establish the political warfare equivalents of present-day organizations such as the Imperial Defence College and the service staff colleges. These political warfare colleges and training establishments would produce the whole-time experts who would eventually be attached to institutions which would be of particular importance in a political warfare struggle with an occupying power. For example I picture the T.U.C. the Newspaper Proprietors' Association, the principal industrial associations, the B.B.C., the nationalized industries, having attached to them small permanent staffs of persons trained in the new form of psychological defence and able to give guidance if an occupation occurred, and training in preparation for this event.

At this stage in my argument, and not for the first time in these reflections, I sense the need to launch a psychological counter-attack against doubts, perhaps even ridicule, in the minds of some readers. Do I hear some one say: "Experts trained at Political Warfare Colleges attached to the T.U.C. or to the Press? What fantasy is this?"

My reply is that such critics are still on the wrong side of the thought barrier in defence matters, because I doubt if any of the critics will take exception to the following statement: "In conventional war, as soon as hostilities begin, the T.U.C. and Press (to take two of my examples) are at once brought into the closest touch with the military authorities, whose job it is to mobilize all the resources of the nation in support of the grand strategy of the war. When in World War II men and women were directed into industry, buildings and land requisitioned, farmers directed what to grow, civilians told what to eat and what to wear, etc., all this was based on military necessity. The Press is censored, and this was happily done in Britain in World War II, on a voluntary basis, but the chief censor was an Admiral."

All I am suggesting in my proposals, or to be more exact in my agenda for an enquiry, is that for the words "military authorities" there be substituted the words "political warfare authorities" and that as World War III in cold form is going on now we should take time by the forelock and make appropriate preparations in case it becomes hot and leads to an occupation of the U.K. as an alternative to being obliterated.

Another objection may be that it looks as if I were proposing the creation of hordes of officials. My reply: "I should anticipate that, taking into account the progressive reduction in the size of the conventional forces, there would be a net saving in man-power."

The trained specialists would be members of a regular service analogous to the Foreign Service, the Fire Service, the Police Service, the Health Service, in which men and women would make their careers. It should be called The Defence Service.

To call it at this stage *The Civil Defence Service* would lead to misunderstanding because *Civil Defence* is at present associated with passive defence against enemy air attack.

In addition to the whole-time personnel of the service, which would be built up to direct the non-violent resistance of the nation, there would be part-time training for every citizen on a voluntary basis.

I attach great importance to this voluntary element in the scheme and I believe that once the general idea of the new policy of defence had been accepted by the nation, hundreds of thousands of citizens would be willing to join the local branch of this organization as volunteers and undertake training in non-violent resistance. "Training?" it may be asked. "What does this mean?" It means, if for the sake of illustration we accept my suggestion that the parliamentary division be adopted as the local unit, that, to take the division I happen to live in, which is Petersfield, the electors would be prepared as to how to behave in the event of an enemy occupation and that in every village there would be a group of people known to be the local leaders and guiding committee of the resistance movement. It is taken as normal that in each constituency there is an organization network to-day for each political party and for civil defence (military form). The political party organizations are in fact bodies engaged in a form of political warfare with each other in a battle of the brains for the allegiance of the minds of the electorate. They conduct the campaign by means of meetings, the distribution of literature, house-to-house canvass and—whist drives and other social occasions! The civil defence people struggle with the same type of problem, substituting exercises in rescue work for social occasions.

The new Defence Service which I envisage being developed would also hold its exercises and manœuvres. Areas and centres of population would be "occupied" by the forces of the small, non-nuclear armed services in order to test out the plans of non-violent defence service in that area. If E.T.O. came into existence and became well organized, inter-national occupation exercises could be tried out. To those to whom all this sounds as improbable and quasi-absurd as space fiction, I must say that military forces hold manœuvres and exercises and unfortunately pay a price in human life and few give the casualties a second thought, and a man-made satellite is going round the earth as I write these words. Let us keep at least an open mind as to what may become accepted as reasonable.

The picture in my mind is that of a defence organization in the psychological field operating amongst all classes of the community on a voluntary basis, trained, organized and exercised by personnel of a whole-term service.

To sum up:

There seem to me to be three stages in the evolution of a comprehensive scheme for the defence of our way of life by non-violent resistance and positive psychological action against Communism. They are:

Stage I. The public debate which may lead to the decision to adopt a totally new basis for a defence strategy. As an initial step in Stage I, I advocate the immediate setting up of a large-scale public enquiry. Since I first made this proposal the Government has created the precedent of appointing a committee of three to report direct to the public about our economic position. This should be the constitutional status of the enquiry into defence.

Stage II. The announcement by the Government in agreement with the Opposition that the new policy had been adopted. Negotiations with our allies to fix a time-table for the key announcement that we intended to abandon the use of nuclear energy for military purposes. It would at this stage become apparent whether our decision would lead to plans for setting up the European Treaty Organization or whether we should be left, for the time being at any rate, "to go it alone".

The formation of the non-violent resistance Defence Service; establishment of staff colleges; educational work in schools.

Stage III. The extension of the scheme to the whole nation. If Stage I began now it might be concluded by 1959. If the policy were adopted in 1959-60, Stage II might be well developed by 1963. Stage II would begin before 1963, perhaps in 1961 and would have no closing period, but the nation should be reasonably well organized by 1968.

A PERSONAL CONCLUSION

A PERSONAL CONCLUSION

IN THE REFLECTIONS on defence in the nuclear age which are recorded in the preceding pages, I approached the problem of defence from the severely practical point of view in order to ascertain whether what the moralists declare to be right may not also be an expedient course of action. A study of this subject would not be complete without some few words about wider considerations than the problem of how to defend our way of life in the United Kingdom. All the signs indicate that man is at a road junction of history, but a junction unlike any he has hitherto reached.

The continuation of the testing of nuclear weapons, a process which shows no signs of coming to an end and will increase as more and more nations are driven to seek possession of these means of defence, may produce deadly consequences to future generations, but, long before the world begins to be peopled by monsters, there will be war and war will be nuclear. A war of this character would end civilization as we know it to-day and do so through unimaginable experiences of human suffering.

The junction which we have reached is unprecedented in character because it marks the point of no return. One road leads to survival, to peace and to a degree of material prosperity and human leisure through the peaceful use of nuclear energy never known to man; the other leads to death and destruction. To-day we are marking time at the junction; perhaps sidling perilously near the turning to death.

Some one, some how, in some way, must change the fatal posture of perilous poise between the choice of route and give a dramatic and inspiring lead towards sanity.

The British people have made notable contributions to the whole content of modern civilization. In government they have done much to develop and spread the institution of parliament; in the production of wealth they were the begetters of the first industrial revolution. By accident—no doubt—they were responsible for the United States of America and, by design, modern India. In defence of liberty in the pre-nuclear age they made immense sacrifices in two great wars. They are indeed a considerable people whose general influence on human history during the past 500 years has been more significant than that of any other national group.

I find myself increasingly driven to the conclusion that destiny has placed an enormous responsibility on the British people at this time. It is hopeless to expect the U.S.A. or the Soviet Union to take a unilateral decision which will break the tension and deadlock between these two giants. For the moment only one other state, Great Britain, has the capacity to produce and stock-pile nuclear weapons. It may be a brief moment. Great Britain is still in every respect, save that of military strength, a Great Power and in terms of world prestige possibly still the greatest of all the Powers. Whatever one may assess the risks to be, there can be no question that a unilateral decision by Great Britain to abandon the use of nuclear energy for military purposes would make a tremendous impact on the world situation and be recognized by our friends, our enemies and the uncommitted nations as an historic decision of extra-ordinary importance.

In this book I have endeavoured to examine the arguments for and against the adoption of this policy by my country. It is not a question about which any individual should have the temerity to assert "I am sure the answer is YES (or NO)". There is nothing technical about the basic elements in this great problem and the opinion of anyone who can read and write and is prepared to think hard about this grave problem is as good as mine.

But I am sure that it is a question which should be urgently examined by some sort of an enquiry staffed by persons with wisdom and imagination and whose standing in the nation will ensure respect for their findings. The enquiry should be in public but as it is important that they should have access to facts known only to government, some parts of its deliberations might have to be held in closed sessions. Whilst reserving my final personal position until the enquiry I ask for has made its report, I have come round to the view that on the facts known to me and after endeavouring to assess the relative dangers of the risks inseparable from our present defence policy and those which seem to arise from the adoption of the alternative policy, I support the idea of changing the basis of our defence strategy from one of violence to one of non-violence. I therefore advocate the implementation of this policy by a declaration (unilateral if need be, if other powers will not join with us) that the U.K. Government as from a date to be announced, will abandon the use of nuclear energy for military purposes. The thought which gave me the final thrust through the thought-barrier separating the mental world of violent defence (in which I have lived and studied these questions for most of my life) to the new world of thought about defence in which violence has no place in major conflicts, is the reflection that by adopting this new policy my country has a duty to take great risks in a supreme effort to save mankind from its impending doom, and that in the words of our poet Milton:

"Let not England forget her precedence in teaching the nations how to live."